WORTH THE WAIT

being an **anomaly** in an immoral world

WORTH THE WAIT

being an **anomaly** in an immoral world

TYLER WALEA AND **KEN GURLEY**

WORD AFLAME PRESS
HAZELWOOD, MO

Worth the Wait: An Anomaly in an Immoral World

By Tyler Walea and Ken Gurley

Published by Word Aflame Press, 8855 Dunn Road, Hazelwood, MO 63042. Printed in the United States of America.

This book is dedicated to all those who made a stand for moral purity in previous generations. Your commitment and example bring hope to a new generation.

CONTENTS

INTRODUCTION

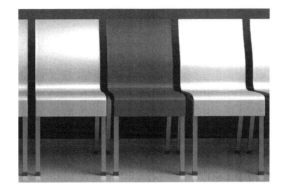

My second daughter was born two months ago, and she taught me a lot about waiting. She was born several weeks early, and after the whirlwind of her complicated birth I spent a lot of time sitting in hospital waiting rooms. My wife and I would wait for this doctor or that specialist. We'd wait to speak with respiratory therapists and nurses. It felt like most of my waking hours in the weeks following her arrival were spent in a hospital chair waiting for someone.

The waiting room on the fourth floor of The Woman's Hospital of Texas, just outside the Newborn Intensive Care Unit, became my sanctuary. I sat for hours in a chair by the window overlooking the hospital's courtyard. I talked to doctors and family members and friends in that chair. More importantly, I talked to God in that chair.

The concept of a waiting room is simple: It's a place to stay until you know what's happening next. It's a quiet place to collect your thoughts, a refuge from the chaos. Just beyond the walls that define the waiting space there are loud operating rooms and brightly lit labs and treatments centers. But there's peace and safety in the waiting room.

If you examine the state of modern culture, you don't have to dig too deeply until you uncover the sense of urgency that characterizes life in the twenty-first century. The immediate rules the day—instant gratification, electronic communication, the incredible weight of "now." The immediate nature of our culture overflows into every area of life, and nowhere has it become more apparent in the lives of young adults than in our relationships.

Low-commitment, high-consequence connections rule the day. Sexual immorality has become an accepted part of life. Somewhere along the way, normal got redefined, the idea of lasting commitments became strange, and life began spinning faster and faster out of control.

I wish life came with waiting rooms. Amid the flow of life's decisions, there should be a place to pause. There should be a refuge. There should be a chair by the window.

If you'll allow me to make a suggestion, I'd like to offer you the six chapters of this book as one of life's waiting rooms. A place to stop. A place to think. A place to consider your commitments.

Pull up a chair, and get comfortable with being weird, because waiting makes you weird. Waiting makes you an anomaly in a society that teaches us to value fitting in. But there is still value in waiting. In a world that would convince you otherwise, waiting is worth it . . . and you are still worth the wait.

Tyler Walea

CHAPTER ONE – WHO TURNED OUT THE LIGHTS?

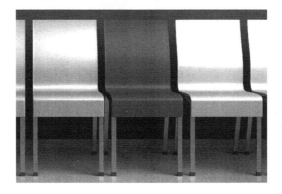

Defining Darkness

"Find people who understand you."

That's the slogan of the Experience Project, an online library of user-submitted life experiences. The website is approaching forty million anonymous posts ranging from hilarious to heartbreaking. The posts are in response to simple prompts like "What did you have for dinner?" or more complex ideas like "I know I'll be alone forever." Buried in the millions of experiences is one post by the user *alienatedvirus* entitled "I Prefer Darkness over Light."

> I prefer darkness over light. The darkness allows me to hide who I am and what I truly feel. In the light all things have a chance to be revealed. Darkness makes it easier to hide. In the dark you cannot see

what is coming next. The darkness is a place where you can lose yourself. Lost in the dark is a great place to be because then you are free from what you were and can be what you want. The darkness is bliss.

Easy to hide. A place where you can lose yourself. Be what you want. Darkness. It's a frightening but accurate description of twenty-first century culture. In modern society the cover and comfort of spiritual darkness has allowed the abnormal to become normal. Things that were once considered sinful are now acceptable. Bizarre behavior is expected and even celebrated. The shocking is no longer shocking.

A simple web search of recent headlines provides enough proof to last ten lifetimes:

"Human trafficking on the rise in Pennsylvania."
"Heroin addiction increasing across the US."
"Abortion rate still increasing among impoverished women."
"Dozens die of overdose as popularity of raves increases."
"Terrorist sleeper cells proliferating in Germany."
Slavery. Drugs. Abortion. Terrorism. Darkness.

Jesus told Nicodemus in John 3:19-20 (NIV), "This is the verdict: Light has come into the world, but men loved darkness instead of light because their deeds were evil. Everyone who does evil hates the light, and will not come into the light for fear that his deeds will be exposed."

It's into this darkness-loving culture that we are called to shine a light. The difficulty is that modern culture is not passive or ineffectual. An increasingly dark society begins to normalize deviant behavior. Evil deeds are expected, faith is questioned, and morality is presented as only one of many paths to fulfillment.

It creates a difficult task for those who are called to be salt and light in a light-hating society. Given time, being immersed in reality can begin to rob the salt of its savor and dim the brightest of lights. That's why the struggle to change our world without allowing the world to change us remains one of our most challenging fights.

We've given it innocuous-sounding names like societal drift or moral decline, but the truth is there is a very real enemy who is out to steal, kill, and destroy everything we value. It is no longer enough to strive to be counter-cultural in our stands on morality. The time to simply "make a stand" or "speak out" against culture has passed; it's time to go to war to set free a generation that is being swallowed by spiritual darkness. And make no mistake, it is a war, and the prisoners do not know they are prisoners.

Swimming in a Cave

Imagine you've just stepped into a cave. The floor, walls, and ceiling are slick black rock. You step deeper inside and light a candle that sends shadows flickering down the black path. As you go deeper, it gets darker. After walking downward for several minutes, past stalactites and stalagmites, you come to a small body of water and the light of your candle reveals small fish rising to the surface and then sinking back below. You kneel for a closer look and realize many of the fish have no eyes. They are swimming up and down, searching for food in absolute darkness, some blind, some entirely eyeless, oblivious to your lone light shining across the surface of the water.

It almost sounds made up, but it's not. *Astyanax mexicanus*, the blind cavefish, has a lightless existence. In any normal lake or pond environment a blind or eyeless fish would quickly become the dinner of a predator. But in an environment that doesn't require sight, the fish thrive, reproduce, and pass on their lack of vision to the next generation.

Modern society is the pond at the bottom of the cave, and people by the billions are swimming in sightless circles, passing their comfort with darkness to a generation that doesn't know what it is to truly see. Most frighteningly, the darkness of the cave has redefined normal. In the cave, blindness is expected. In the cave, sight is an anomaly. In the cave, everyone grows comfortable with the dark.

Darkness has become a frightening, new kind of normal, and we are all in this cave together. For years we played the card of "us," the church, and "them," the world, as if we were somehow entirely insulated from society's flaws. The truth is, while we may with God's help be immune to culture, we are still immersed in it. We must, therefore, somehow find it in our hearts to live holy, to live pure, and to live right while everything around us invites us to close our eyes and give in to a lightless existence.

We understand that it is possible to live seeing in a sightless world. It is possible to walk circumspectly, as Paul directed us in Ephesians 5:15-16, wisely keeping our eyes open because the day is evil. He goes on to remind us one chapter later, in Ephesians 6:12, that we don't wrestle against flesh and blood, but against principalities, powers, rulers of the darkness of this world, and spiritual wickedness in high places. We understand that the fight for our collective future is not a natural one, but a spiritual one. The problem, however, is that our greatest weakness tends to invite our most persistent battle. And when it comes to weakness, the fact that we're made up of an enormous amount of flesh makes us weakest of all. We're fighting a fight in our bodies, but it's not just our bodies that we're fighting. We're warring with powers, and darkness, and spiritual wickedness that wants to destroy not only our bodies, but also our souls.

The effect of long-term cave dwelling on our flesh is easily seen. It shows up in our music, our media, our television shows, and movies. Biblical directives to think on good things and to set no evil thing before our eyes are challenged every morning before breakfast. It's heard in conversations in the hallways of our schools and elevated in the classrooms of our greatest universities. It's even in the actions of many who say they are Christians but live as if God is a creature from a fairy tale. Above all, it's seen in the context of our behavior, our conversations, and our relationships with others.

Relationships are interesting things. In no other area of life is our soul and our body so connected as in our relationships. You've probably heard dozens of people use phrases like "soul connection" or "it's not just physical," when discussing sex. Sexuality does not stop at the physical. That is the power of relationships. It impacts the emotions and the spirit on an even more permanent basis than the physical. Perhaps that's why the enemy of our souls comes against our bodies so relentlessly through the sin of lust and the desire for sex.

Sex Gone Wrong

It's no secret that we have a sex problem. Studies and statistics abound that prove we have a sex problem that is not going away on its own. Sex is consistently portrayed in modern media as being primarily recreational. The Association for Psychological Science recently released a study that says at least 85 percent of movies released in a year have significant sexual content. The few minutes of screen time portray a fantasy but fail to follow up with the reality. They don't show the pain, the emotional scars, or the bruised spirits left in the wake of momentary relationships that need more than time and distance to be healed.

Dr. Archibald D. Hart says in *Healing Life's Hidden Addictions*, "The most powerful force in the physical world is not the nuclear bomb–but sex! Addictions to alcohol and cocaine may be major problems for our age, but they pale into insignificance when compared with the ravages of sex gone wrong."

If sex can go right, it can also go wrong. And the "wrongs" of sex are what we rarely talk about or see played out to their true end on one-hour television dramas.

Unwanted Pregnancies

Although the birth rate among teens has dropped to a sixty-year low, consider these facts:

Every sixty-four seconds a baby is born to a teenaged mother. Every five minutes a baby is born to a teenaged mother who already has another child. One million teen women get pregnant each year. Sixty-five percent of teenaged mothers are unmarried. Seventy-eight percent of teen pregnancies are unplanned. (Source: Anderson, p. 120, Alan Guttmacher Institute, Teen Sex and Pregnancy.)

It's sex gone wrong.

Abortions

In the past forty years, about forty million unborn children have been legally aborted in the United States. Every twenty seconds, two lives are taken by abortion. The first is the unborn child. The second is abortion's forgotten victim—the mother who has to live with memories for a lifetime.

It's sex gone wrong.

Sexually Transmitted Diseases

In 1972, the year before the US Supreme Court's landmark abortion ruling in *Roe v. Wade*, there were only two sexually transmitted diseases (STDs) at epidemic levels. Today, there are at least twenty active STDs. A third of all Americans over the age of ten have one or more of these diseases. An estimated sixty-five million Americans are afflicted with at least one of these incurable diseases that can lead to infertility, miscarriages, stillbirths, mother-to-infant infections, and cancer. And, sadly enough, each year twelve to fifteen million new cases are reported. (Mark Tapscott, director of Center for Media and Public Policy at the Heritage Foundation).

It's sex gone wrong.

Emotional Trauma

Sex outside of marriage carries a high emotional price tag. Couples engaging in premarital sex quite often think the relationship is much deeper than what it is. They find out how shallow it is soon enough when the hurt comes: guilt, fear, heartbreak, misunderstanding, loss of identity and personal values, and a fracturing of the soul.

It's sex gone wrong.

The fact that society is getting increasingly dark is inarguable. But if sex and society can go wrong, they can also go right. Let's turn on the light, shall we?

A Better Plan

God has a better plan.

Say it aloud. Seriously. Wherever you are right now, say it aloud.

God. Has. A. Better. Plan.

Sometimes you have to remind yourself of that. Otherwise, you'll get stuck in the rut of believing the chaos and darkness that so often surrounds us is all there is.

God has a plan for your life. God has a plan for your talents and giftings and abilities. God has a plan for your relationships and for the family you'll someday have. And yes, God even has a plan for sex.

Look down the road and dream a bit. Imagine the married version of you. Imagine a couple of kids on a swing in the backyard. Imagine the minivan. Yes, go ahead and imagine the minivan. Here's the thing. We tend to make life decisions based on the "us" of the next ten minutes rather than the "us" of the next ten years. God's plan looks even further than that.

Most individuals' regrets revolve around making decisions with short-term thinking that had long-term consequences. The twenty-year-old version of you doesn't realize that the thirty-year-old version of you with a family will have to live with the choices you made ten years earlier. And life is full of choices.

The familiar Bible story of Daniel in Babylon is a story of a man with a choice to make. He was a stranger to the society that was his home from his youth to late adulthood. Again and again, he was given opportunity for advancement and given the chance to fit in. It's a biblical picture of the same choice that is given daily to each of us. You can choose to fit into the mold of culture. You can choose to fly below the radar, keeping your beliefs and convictions to yourself. Or you can choose to be an anomaly. You can say, like Daniel, I'd rather be a Jewish prisoner than a king of Babylon. I'd rather suffer for being who I am than live a lie and pretend to be something I am not.

Why would you choose the more difficult road, Daniel? Because this is not me. These aren't my clothes, this isn't my food. I have different laws. I have different customs. I don't belong here. So I'll suffer through the shame of imprisonment before I'll betray who I am.

The Mole People

It sounds like the stuff of urban legend. Far below the streets of New York City, thousands of people live in abandoned tunnels and chambers of the NYC subway system. Called the "Mole People," they live mostly in darkness, a few venturing above ground at night to secure food and medical supplies. Jennifer Toth profiled the subculture a few years ago in an extensively researched book, and her research uncovered a thriving culture that had adapted to life beneath the city. The normal world is just above their heads. Restaurants and shops line the streets. Children play in the sunlight. Families gather and discuss their days and their plans. Below them, the mole people pick their way through the dark tunnels of a life that somehow accepted darkness and loneliness as normal.

In some ways it's a vivid picture of life in this world—the dark, the danger, the community, evading the law. Like spiritual mole people, we sometimes find ourselves living below our God-intended "normal." Just a little higher above us is the life that we should be living. But we see others around us living in darkness, and the darkness becomes normal. Sexual immorality becomes normal. Sin becomes normal. Wrong decisions become normal.

Jesus said to Nicodemus, "This is the verdict: Light has come into the world, but men loved darkness instead of light because their deeds were evil. Everyone who does evil hates the light, and will not come into the light for fear that his deeds will be exposed."

So what's the point? Don't buy into the culture that says dark is normal and light is to be feared. We are not mole people. We are citizens of a different kingdom. Society does not value or expect sexual purity, but it remains a priority with those who serve God. Purity is not normal. But we were never supposed to be normal.

Culture Crush

So where to from here? We are called to be in the world but not of the world, to be immersed in culture while remaining immune to it. When our lives reflect that, we become the living witnesses that the Word of God calls us to be. When the darkness of culture begins to creep into our thinking, however, we tend to move in one of three directions:

Carnality (In the world and of the world) If we're not careful, we can find ourselves consumed with carnal thinking. When we grow accustomed to the dark, our thoughts often begin reflecting the thought process of the world around us rather than the Spirit inside us. Carnal things become the source of our joy, and we drift away from the purpose God intended for us to possess.

Seclusion (Not in the world, and not of the world) Moving in the opposite direction, the darkness can become so overwhelming that we retreat in fear. We don't become like the world, but we also fail to change the world because we've withdrawn from it. The biblical call to "come out from among them" is a call to a life of difference, not distance.

Hypocrisy (Not in the world, but still of the world) To be very blunt, that's when we hide on church pews. We attend Sunday school and youth service, and then go do the wrong thing afterwards. We have a church language, but we also have an outside-church language. We have a church lifestyle and an outside-church lifestyle.

When we are carnal, secluded, or hypocritical, we miss the calling and purpose God has for our life. When that happens, the light inside us remains hidden and darkness reigns.

The place we draw the line is the place we fight the battle. Our most valuable boundaries will always be our greatest battlegrounds. So what if we decided today that the fight is worth it? What if we decided that fighting the darkness of culture is worth the struggle? What if we decided that the battleground of purity is ground that's too important to give away?

Why does it matter? Because 7,700 teens lose their virginity each day in America. Sometimes the numbers seem so overwhelming that teens feel like "everybody is doing it." According to a survey in *Seventeen* magazine, 75 percent of teens believe that most of their peers are having sex. That is the frightening, new normal of the twenty-first century. If that's the cultural norm, perhaps it's time to make a counter-cultural commitment. Maybe it's time to be the kind of "different" that makes people ask questions.

Our culture does not tolerate neutrality. We will either do something to the world or the world will do something to us. So, moving forward, we need to get comfortable with different. Get comfortable with living outside the lines drawn by media, movies, and music. Get comfortable with speaking up. Get comfortable with the idea that, when we make commitments, we'll actually talk about them. We won't live ashamed. We won't live quietly. We will be an anomaly.

And we can be perfectly fine with that.

Follow-Up Questions:

1. In John 3:19-20, what did Jesus tell Nicodemus is the reason human beings love darkness?

   _____

   _____

   _____

2. In Ephesians 5:15-16, why does Paul tell us to redeem the time?

   _____

   _____

   _____

3. What is meant by the sentence, "Every twenty seconds, two lives are taken by abortion"?

   _____

   _____

   _____

4. How did Daniel choose to be an anomaly rather than flying below the radar?

   _____

   _____

   _____

5. When the darkness of culture begins to creep in to our thinking, in what three directions do we tend to move?

   _____

   _____

   _____

Journal Your Thoughts:

As you work through this chapter, journal your thoughts about being a light in a dark world.

_____

_____

_____

_____

_____

_____

CHAPTER TWO—
THE CASE FOR ABSTINENCE

"Everyone's doing it!"

That's what they tell at public schools. In assembly programs, health and sociology classes, and in any other forum available, the mantra of the majority is always the same: "Water flows downhill and people will have sex."

The standard approach goes like this:

- Human beings are sexual creatures with sex organs and are thus designed to have sexual relationships.
- Sex is normal, expected, and appropriate for all humans.
- Sex should be practiced in a responsible, safe manner.

Left unsaid in this approach is that having sex is not merely a physical act, but affects the whole person—emotionally, mentally, socially, and spiritually—and affects others not for the moment, but for ages to come. Yet, these aspects of sexual relationships are, for the most part, absent from the majority mindset.

The media proclaims that everyone is having sex. Take nearly any form of media—music, music videos, television, magazines, social media, Internet sites, and the message remains the same: "Everyone is doing it!"

Sexual innuendos and encounters are at an all-time high on television—yes, even network primetime television—and these reinforce the inevitable conclusion that sex is normal and expected ("Is There an Epidemic of Nudity on Prime Time TV?," *TIME*, June 10, 2013).

Does it affect behavior? One research report after another shows that what is seen on television affects mindsets and behaviors (e.g., "TV's Newest Target: Teen Sexual Exploitation, Parent's Television Council).

Jeremiah said it best, "Mine eye affecteth mine heart" (Lamentations 3:51). What we see, knowingly or unknowingly, affects our thoughts, our speech, and our behavior.

Via social media, "sexting" became a teen and young adult fad. The convergence of digital media with smart phones proved an opportunity to advance the idea that normal dating relationships included salacious texts and photos. News stories regularly report how such practices have gone bad. Nevertheless, the underlying premise is that all sex is normal and expected.

To say that music and music videos have become more sexually-charged is to state the obvious. Secular artists seem to compete with lyrics and performances to out-shock the audience. In certain genres of music, profanity is so common that it's not uncommon to have hundreds of curse words per album. In a sick society where four-letter-words are common, it's odd that the most uncomfortable word for many has six letters: "virgin."

Before we leave media, it may be good to examine the simple premise of this from their perspective: "Sex sells." Advertisers and producers find that sexually-charged products attract greater attention amongst the majority of targeted consumers. Consequently, the media will, quite possibly, have greater sexual overtones in the future.

Complicit in this majority mindset that sex is normal and expected is a willing governmental system that advocates and promotes this understanding. Funding dollars pour into a traditional "comprehensive sex education" curriculum which may or may not include a discussion of abstinence. Of the programs that present abstinence as the most effective method of preventing unintended pregnancies and sexually transmitted diseases (STDs), abstinence is presented as least plausible because of the underlying premise that sex is normal and expected. Federal funding for abstinence-only curricula was at one time robust but has been struggling in recent years.

With the everyone's-doing-it mindset so entrenched in a wide spectrum of influential institutions, it's little wonder that the majority believe this to be accepted fact. Yet, there are two things quite often overlooked: first, not everyone is doing it;

and second, those engaging in premarital sex experience significant consequences.

Everybody Is NOT Doing It.

Granted there are many people engaging in premarital sex. Depending upon which survey is cited, it is safe to say that in recent years the majority of unwed teens and young adults have engaged in premarital sex. The definition of sex has also steadily grown more permissive.

There are many, however, who do not engage in premarital sex. Again, depending upon which set of surveys you examine, the numbers vary. For example, the 2011 Center for Disease Control report on sexuality reported 27 percent of men and 29 percent of women ages 15-24 have never had sexual intercourse. Each year in America, there are thousands of people getting married who have never had sex.

So, not everyone is doing it. Yet, a word of caution is probably appropriate. In "(Almost) Everyone's Doing It" found in *RELEVANT*, a Christian magazine, the author noted that the rates of premarital sex do not differ much from all unmarried young adults ages 18-29 (88 percent) and those who identify themselves as Christians (80 percent). Extend the age range to all single adults who profess to be Christians and one study shows that nine in ten are "sexual atheists," meaning that there is no difference in sexual practices between supposed believers and non-believers (Study done by *www. ChristianMingle*, reported in *www.Christian Post*, April 10, 2014).

Everyone may not be doing it, but shouldn't we expect that Christians would fare much better in such studies?

Consequences

We will deal more specifically with the high costs of premarital sex in the next section, but it's worthy to note here an instance where the government-sponsored media took note of the immense costs associated with sexual promiscuity.

PBS ran a special documentary contrary to the prevalent worldview on sexuality a few years ago called "The Lost Children of Rockdale County." Its content proved to be a wake-up call for those in America who could be stirred from slumber.

Conyers, Georgia, is an affluent Atlanta suburb located in Rockdale County. On the surface, it is an ideal place to call home — good shopping, restaurants, churches, schools, and homes. Behind the scenes, things were not nearly so idyllic.

The documentary told the story of an odd outbreak of syphilis in the teens of this community. Over fifty teens were involved in extreme sexual behavior. Some of these teens had between twenty and fifty partners. Sexually transmitted diseases — one of the consequences of promiscuous sex — were running rampant amongst the group. The townsfolk and parents were oblivious to what was happening.

One of the more touching interviews involved three Christian girls who were virgins and trying to stay that way. These girls told the researchers how they faced ridicule, lies, and mockeries from their peers. Each had been scorned for trying to remain sexually pure. In spite of this persecution, they clung to their beliefs and their hopes of remaining sexually pure. In such an environment, it takes great courage to live morally pure.

Maybe you can relate to these girls. Maybe your classmates and coworkers boast of their sexual activities. You may feel isolated and alone. One of the girls interviewed in Rockdale County said, "It really is hard, you know, when you try to be good, and then people want to always tar you and say, 'Oh, no. You're a hypocrite,' you know? It's really hard. . . . "

It's not easy to be different. Nor is it easy to remain sexually pure. That's why we need to know the straight facts about abstinence—abstaining from sex until marriage. Abstinence may be in the minority, but it has greater benefits than the promiscuity practiced by the majority.

Kim's Story

The phone rang at New Beginnings, a care center for unwed mothers located in lovely Tupelo, Mississippi. Debbie, the manager, answered the phone. The frightened voice on the other end of the line belonged to a woman who identified herself as Kim, an eighteen-year-old girl from upstate New York.

After this and other phone conversations, the story of her life emerged. Her father died when she was twelve years of age. Two years later her mother had remarried, and almost immediately her stepfather began sexually molesting her. Debbie's heart went out to this young lady. The sorrow of losing a father was only compounded by the actions of her stepfather.

The story gushed out. Kim's mother worked nights and she and her step-father were home alone. This is when the abuse began. He threatened to kill her if she ever told anyone.

On a certain night, she found the courage to resist him. He accused her of seeing someone else and beat her so severely that she missed school for a week. The reason for her new found courage was simple, but painful: she was pregnant with her stepfather's child.

"He doesn't know," she told Debbie, "and I'm afraid he's going to hurt me."

Debbie did what God has gifted her to do. She began helping Kim see a future beyond this present tragedy. She offered to purchase an airline ticket to fly Kim to New Beginnings where they could discuss her options and view the facility. Kim told Debbie that she would hear back from her within sixteen days.

"Sixteen days?" asked Debbie.

"Yes," responded Kim. "That's when I need to let the abortion clinic know whether I will have an abortion or opt for keeping the child."

The phone calls ended. A week passed in silence. Debbie thought about Kim a lot. She prayed for her and hoped that she would hear from her. She did— sort of.

A week later, Debbie answered the phone. On the other end was a woman who at first identified herself as Kim. Then, she said, "My real name is Linda. I am thirty-two years old, I am married, and I have two children. I was pregnant by my stepfather when I was eighteen, but I chose an abortion. I have had emotional problems since that time. I am currently in counseling and it is helping, but this is not the first time I have called someone like this. I am so tormented by having had an abortion that I try to go back in my mind and do it over. I wish so badly that I had made the right decision then, so I convince myself that I am eighteen again and that I am pregnant, but this time I choose to have the baby and place it for adoption. I'm sorry for taking your time."

Debbie sat in stunned silence. She knew that many women who choose abortions experience emotional trauma. That a woman could still be so severely haunted by phantoms of her past fourteen years later surprised her. She assured Linda that she and others were praying for her and the phone call ended.

The caller's words are chilling in themselves, "I try to go back in my mind and do it over." Phantoms from the past have a way of returning when they're least expected.

The Minority Report

God has always been comfortable with the minority opinion. Elijah stood alone against an assortment of 850 false prophets—but Elijah's God came through at Mount Carmel. In the same sense, a host of people may say that casual sex is okay and expected. But being in the majority doesn't make it right.

God made sexual relations for a marriage between a man and woman. Biblically, sex between unmarried people is not called normal but sinful. Specifically, sexual relations before marriage is called fornication, and the person who commits fornication sins against his own body, the temple of the Holy Ghost (I Corinthians 6:18).

God promises to judge sexual sin including fornication, adultery, and homosexuality (Hebrews 13:4; I Corinthians 6:9, 10). It is interesting to note that our word "pornography" also comes from the same root word found in fornication. Actual sexual sins are linked with imagined ones. Jesus taught against the sin of adultery in His Sermon on the Mount and then went further saying that whoever looked on a woman in lust commits adultery in his heart (Matthew 5:28). The mind and the body are unbreakably bound together.

There are any number of reasons why it is good to abstain from sex until marriage. But, let's review five of the reasons why abstinence is a better choice.

Some Positive Reasons for Abstinence

There are numerous reasons for saving sex for marriage. Let's elevate five that focus on the future.

Abstinence heightens the chance of marrying the right person. The Bible portrays sin as a "work of darkness." All sin blinds, but sexual sin really turns the lights off! When sex enters into a dating relationship, the individuals stop seeing clearly. They can't discern between right and wrong in the moral sense, and they sure can't tell whether this is the right person to marry.

In the United States each year, more than 200,000 marriages end before the couple's second anniversary. Sexual activity prior to marriage can obscure the choice of a mate (Dr. Neil Clark Warren, *Finding the Love of Your Life*, p. 4).

A young couple was asked recently why they chose to remain pure before their marriage. The man responded, "My sexual purity was the most precious gift that I could give my bride-to-be. Our wedding night was the moment to celebrate the wait!"

Abstinence avoids the complications associated with premarital sex. The list is almost endless—disease, emotional upheaval, unintended pregnancies, poverty, and the list goes on.

"Most young people," according to the Center for Disease Control's Sexual Risk Behavior for 2011, "engage in sexual risk behaviors that can result in unintended health outcomes." The report lists some supporting facts:

- 47.4 percent of high school students have had sexual intercourse.
- 15.3 percent of high school students had sex with four or more people.
- Nearly half of the nineteen million newly reported cases of sexually transmitted diseases are among young people aged fifteen to twenty-four.
- More than 400,000 teen girls (fifteen to nineteen) gave birth in 2009.

The world's answer to such matters is a condom. But a piece of latex rubber does not always prevent pregnancies and it certainly can't protect against all sexually transmitted diseases. Even if a condom provided protection against these, it provides no protection for the human heart. The loss of self-esteem, guilt, and shame associated with such acts can last a long time.

Abstinence enhances the possibility of good education and careers. Studies show that the longer a person waits to get married and then sexually active, the less chance that the person will be divorced. More time can be devoted to schooling and preparation for life. In other words, time is on your side when you wait to get married.

In the United States, the average age for women getting married the first time is 26.9 and for men it's 29.8 (Pew Research Center 2011). This gives you time to get a good education and establish your career or calling. The world is not passing you by.

Abstinence brings greater marital satisfaction. When people wait longer to get married and are getting married for the right reasons, it follows that their marriages will be stronger. However, when premarital sex leads a person into marriage, the necessary climate of trust and respect often goes lacking.

Dr. Bill Maier from Focus on the Family responded to a woman who wrote to him saying she was having trouble in her marriage. She admitted that prior to getting married, she and her husband had had sex and she got pregnant. This complicated their marriage.

Maier responded:

> *"In today's world, many so-called 'experts' deny that there are moral or spiritual ramifications to premarital sex. But it's obvious from your e-mail that those 'experts' have it all wrong.*
>
> *"God's created intent for human sexuality is very clear. It is a wonderful gift which brings men and women together emotionally and spiritually. But He designed that gift to be expressed in a life-long marital commitment. When we ignore His design, we often reap a harvest of pain and suffering."*
>
> (Dr. Bill Maier, Focus on the Family website)

Suspicion, distrust, and jealousy can be sown into a marriage because of the emotional baggage carried into the marriage through premarital sex. Abstinence helps to prevent this from happening.

Abstinence promotes a good example to the next generation. Right living is better "caught" than taught. When one generation models sexual purity, it preserves the future of the next generation.

The example of David's sin with Bathsheba lived on in succeeding generations: his son Amnon raped his half-sister Tamar, his son Absalom killed Amnon and tried to overthrow David, and his son Adonijah tried to scheme his way to the throne. David's sin affected not just himself, but his entire family for generations.

The two greatest influences in the lives of the Millennial Generation are parents first and religion second. Obviously, the example set by parents will help shape the children.

Some Negative Strikes against Premarital Sex

Premarital sex has a lot of strikes against it.

Whereas abstinence can keep couples together, premarital sex can break them apart. Those who "give in" usually "give up" their relationships.

Years ago, a woman sent a poem to newspaper columnist Ann Landers that went like this:

> *I met him. I liked him.*
> *I liked him. I loved him.*
> *I let him. I lost him.*

A man read it and sent his own version of the poem to the same columnist.

> *I saw her. I liked her.*
> *I loved her. I wanted her.*
> *I asked her. She said, "No!"*
> *I married her. After 60 years, I still have her.*

Premarital sex also increases the risk of later divorce and extramarital affairs. Patterns laid down prior to marriage are hard to break after the knot is tied. Abstinence leads to more stable marriages; premarital sex leads to less stable marriages ("Premarital Sex and Greater Risk of Divorce," Glenn Stanton, Focus on the Family Findings, April 2011).

Premarital sex also dramatically affects the quality of a person's lifestyle and that of the next generation. Unintended pregnancy is the leading cause of school dropouts amongst teen girls. Less than 2 percent of teen mothers who drop out of high school will go on to finish school and get a college degree by the age of thirty ("Teen Pregnancy & High School Dropout Report, America's Promise Alliance, June 20, 2012).

Children raised in single-parent homes are far more likely to " . . . experience violence, commit suicide, continue a cycle of poverty, become drug dependent, commit a crime, or perform below his peers in education" (Kathryn Wall, *News Leader*, "Statistics Reveal Stark Challenges For Children Raised in One-Parent Homes," November 24, 2012). Certainly not all premarital sex will result in such dire conditions, yet it heightens the likelihood of this being the result.

Having seen some of the positives of abstinence and the negatives of premarital sex, it is easy to understand why God's Word teaches that premarital sex is not in God's will. God wants the best for our lives (Jeremiah 29:11). Saving sex for marriage is smart, right, and worth the wait.

Andrea's Story

It wasn't what you would call a godly home. Andrea's mother was the daughter of a preacher, but somehow things slipped in her relationship with God. Andrea became a casualty, a statistic of being the daughter of an absent father.

When Andrea was eleven years of age, her parents divorced. Since then, she could count on one hand the times she had seen her father. Her father found another woman and her mother moved her boyfriend into the house. Although Andrea had both an older and a younger sister, she felt lonely and unloved.

While still in her teens, Andrea found someone to love her. After dating a month, he proposed to her. Three months into their dating relationship, they went to a motel and Andrea gave herself completely to him. Less than two months later, Andrea's older sister also lost her virginity—two girls looking for love.

The relationship lasted about a year. Then, it resumed again a few months later for a short time. It was long enough, however, for Andrea to realize that she had conceived and she was pregnant.

She called her former boyfriend to tell him the news. He showed up at her house and promised to stand by her. His tune changed within a week and soon he was encouraging her to seek an abortion before anyone found out. Andrea refused to do this and realized that she had forever said goodbye to this former boyfriend, the father of her unborn child.

The week seemed frozen, the days passed glacially. Andrea had discovered she was pregnant on Wednesday. By Sunday, her conscience was killing her. She went to church and with a nudge from God; she couldn't hide the truth any longer. She told her mother that she was expecting and together they went and told the pastor's wife.

New Beginnings accepted Andrea in their care. There, she learned the value of praying and reading her Bible each night. While waiting for her baby to be born, she busied herself with figuring out how she got into such a mess and how to avoid it in the future.

Word came to her while she was there that some changes were taking place back at home. Her mother told her boyfriend to leave. Andrea's younger sister was asked at school to write about her hero. She chose Andrea for making a decision to keep the child. She also told Andrea that she was making a commitment to sexual purity.

While Andrea doesn't feel like a hero, she has found love. She found the One who calls Himself love in the Bible. She found that He hears, He cares, and He answers prayer.

Making Your Own Stand for Abstinence

Your body is God's temple, but coexisting in the same temple is your own human will.

God created us with the ability to reason, perceive, and to choose. So powerful are these abilities that we can accept or reject our Creator's will for our life. God wants us to grow in knowledge and in His likeness (Ephesians 4:11-24). Yet, we have the power of choice and can choose to resist His purpose for our lives.

The Ties That Bind

"Sin," said Victor Hugo, "is like gravity." Its invisible grip pulls us steadily downward and prevents us from soaring into heavenly places.

In Jonathan Swift's classic tale of *Gulliver's Travels*, we read how the tiny population of Lilliput tied Gulliver as he lay unconscious. They looped many tiny threads over him until they completely immobilized him. In the same sense, it is the cumulative effect of earthly ties that render us earth-bound. Let's look at a few of these earthly ties.

Lust. Paul told Timothy to "flee youthful lusts" (II Timothy 2:22). Some sins obviously entice certain age groups. One preacher said, "Greed is an old man's sin while lust is a young man's sin." In our youth, we can allow lust to gain a powerful hold on us or we can sever it.

What is lust? Lust is a desire to gratify the senses. "Youthful lusts" call attention to excessive sexual desires. In the Greek, it simply means "over passion" or a burning sexual desire. Fleshly lusts are part of the world's system (I John 2:16-17) and they war against our souls (I Peter 2:11) by enticing us to sin (James 1:14-15). Sexual lust draws us away from God's best in our lives.

Sensual Imaginations. Before the body becomes sexually impure the mind must first be defiled. This occurs through thoughts, or what the Bible calls "imaginations" (Romans 1:21).

The mind is our most important "sexual organ." Jesus taught that sexual imaginations precede the sexual act (Matthew 5:27-28). In the private dressing room of our mind, we can "try on" various sexual activities. Here we can fantasize and imagine what a sexual encounter will be like.

The mind though is not as private as we think. God sees our thoughts and imaginations (Jeremiah 17:10; Genesis 6:5). Not only does God see it, others will eventually see it.

Solomon said, "Keep thy heart with all diligence; for out of it are the issues of life" (Proverbs 4:23). What is in your heart will eventually flow in full view of others. Yesterday's imaginations are today's actions.

It's important to understand the "triggers" for lustful thoughts and sinful imaginations. It could be as simple as the music we hear, the media we watch, the clothes we wear, or the company we keep.

Friends. It is impossible to overestimate the power of friends—for good or bad. Godly company brings out the best in our lives; ungodly company calls out the worst.

The Power That Sets Free

In contrast to earthly ties that pull us downward, heavenly ties pull us upward. One meaning of the word "holy" is to be "earth-free." Sin is like gravity; but holiness defies gravity. The power to live holy can be found in several things:

Praying in the Spirit. It's worth remembering that one way Daniel lived pure in a strange land is that he kept his windows open toward Jerusalem. Before those perpetually open windows he prayed and cried out to God. Through the power of prayer, we can withstand the Evil One and his desires for our lives.

Temptation is like a conversation going on inside of our head. When we pray, we invite the voice of the Lord into the conversation. For prayer is not simply a one-sided recitation to God; He speaks as well. And when we don't know how to pray as we should, the Bible says, the Spirit makes intercession for us (Romans 8:26).

Skillfully using the Word of God. The Word of God is likened to a sword in the believer's armory. To be effective, it must be used. We can commit to memory the Scriptures concerning living a godly, overcoming life. We can quote them to ourselves, to others, and most of all to the Tempter when he comes.

Build strong relationships. Whom the enemy targets, he isolates. People who have premarital sex are quite often seeking relationships they don't have in their lives. A strong relationship with parents helps to prevent premarital sex and other destructive lifestyles. The Bible says, "iron sharpeneth iron" (Proverbs 27:17). Our parents' convictions and insights may serve to sharpen us. If we let them, they can assist us in setting goals in dating and vocations.

Terri Fisher, a psychology professor at Ohio State University says, "Children who readily discuss sex with parents have values more similar to the parents than do those who have little family communication" (Quoted by Barry and Carol St. Clair, *Talking with Your Kids about Love, Sex, and Dating*, p. 16).

Also, we can build strong relationships within our youth group. When we drift away from those who are seeking God, we reveal that we're seeking something other than God.

Observe modest behavior and dress. Paul said that the "body is not for fornication, but for the Lord" (I Corinthians 6:13). Thus, our dress may reflect who owns our life. A believer should dress modestly and discreetly (I Timothy 2:9).

Sight arouses a man's passion while touch incites that of a woman. Not coincidentally, Scripture emphasizes a woman's dress more than that of a man's. Appearance and behavior do matter to God.

Your Personal Stand

God gave us the power of choice. We can choose to put "SELF" on the throne of our heart or we can choose to place "GOD" in that rightful place. If we choose to follow our selfish desires then we quite possibly will experience the consequences of sexual sin. If we choose godly desires, we will escape many of those harmful consequences and will experience many of His blessings.

We can make this stand only for ourselves. We can determine to follow Jesus and to not turn back.

For hundreds of years, Rome celebrated extravagant games that quite often ended in bloodshed and death. On the Coliseum's arena, gladiators fought to the death, Christians were executed and tens of thousands of Roman spectators rejoiced in the spectacle until . . .

Until one man, Telemachus, ended the games. He came to Rome and followed the crowds to the Coliseum. He watched as the gladiators fought. He beheld the bloodthirsty cries from the spectators. Telemachus was appalled and immediately acted. He took a stand.

Telemachus raced down the stands and leaped onto the arena floor. He stood between the dueling gladiators and cried out for them to stop. He pled with them to show mercy. The crowd hurled insults down on Telemachus. Some began to throw stones at him. One gladiator finally ran him through with a sword.

Telemachus died taking a stand against the slaughter that had gone on for years. In so doing, he achieved what was thought impossible. When news of his fateful stand spread throughout the Roman Empire, the upheaval was so strong that the games were forever stopped.

The entire world waits for someone to take a similar stand. Will that someone be you?

Follow-Up Questions:

1. How does one's eye affect one's heart, as presented in Lamentations 3:51?

_____

_____

_____

2. What is the meaning of this sentence: In a sick society where four-letter words are common, it's odd that the most uncomfortable word for many people has six letters: "virgin"?

_____

_____

_____

3. How did Elijah prove that being in the majority doesn't necessarily make it right?

_____

_____

_____

4. What are five reasons why abstinence is a better choice?

_____

_____

_____

_____

_____

5. What four things can help us live holy and "earth-free"?

_____

_____

_____

_____

Journal Your Thoughts:

After having read and studied this chapter, journal your thoughts about the importance of being an anomaly in an ungodly culture.

_____

_____

_____

_____

_____

_____

_____

_____

_____

_____

_____

_____

_____

_____

_____

_____

_____

_____

_____

_____

_____

_____

_____

_____

_____

CHAPTER THREE— RESISTING TEMPTATION

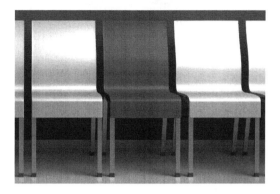

Nearly five hundred years ago, a Spanish conquistador searched what is now the southwestern United States for the famed Seven Cities of Gold. This search party became the first non-Native Americans to see the Grand Canyon. For thousands of years prior to this, Native Americans had lived in and around this gorge carved by the Colorado River.

The canyon is some 277 miles long and up to eighteen miles wide. Grand Canyon National Park is one of the most popular tourist destinations in the United States with millions of visitors coming each year. Where people peer from the canyon rim into its depths, it is around six thousand feet from the rim to the base of the canyon.

The Grand Canyon is old, popular, and dangerous.

In their book, *Over the Edge: Death in the Grand Canyon* (Puma Press, 2001), Michael P. Ghiglieri and Thomas M. Myers chronicle the hundreds of deaths that have occurred in the Grand Canyon over the past hundred years. Flight accidents, rockslides, drownings, and dehydration have caused many of the deaths. One cause of death, regrettably, is also common—carelessness.

Dozens of people have accidentally fallen from the rim of the canyon. Some of these were having photos taken and they got close to the rim and pretended to fall—only to find that pretense so close to the edge is dangerous. Better to steer clear of the abyss than to play alongside it.

Like the canyon, temptation is old, popular, and dangerous. Unlike the Grand Canyon, it seems that everyone wants to jump off of temptation's cliffs.

The problem of temptation extends for all of man's history. The Garden of Eden did not seem a likely place for temptation to make its first appearance. After all, what more could this first couple in Scripture want? In Paradise only one thing was forbidden Adam and Eve and . . . you guessed it, that's what they wanted. Or, at least, that's what they thought they wanted.

It's the Tempter's ongoing business to make us feel like we're missing out—that somehow God has deprived us. The fear of missing out is a favored, frequently-used tool of the enemy. If the Tempter can make us feel less than favored, he can quite often destroy hope—something he fears.

Temptation's life span extends to the present and it has never been more treacherous.

Sights and Sounds

Temptation gains access through one or more human senses: sight, sound, touch, smell, or taste. As the Tempter's encounter with Eve witnesses, quite often sight and sound are the primary routes used to unleash a deluge of hurt and shame in our lives.

Satan tempted Adam and Eve with sight: "When the woman saw that the tree was good for food . . . she took of its fruit and ate" (Genesis 3:6, NKJV). Scripture calls visual temptations the "lust of the eye" (I John 2:16).

Social scientists say we live in a postmodern age. One of the qualities of postmodernism is a marked shift from the written and spoken word to visual media. With the advent of digital media, the number of photos each year grows ever larger.

"Every two minutes," cited the researchers at *1000memories. com*, "we snap as many photos as the whole of humanity took in the 1800s." The same group estimates that in the year of 2013, over one trillion photos were taken in the world. Add to this number of photos the many videos, ranging from a few seconds to a few hours, produced by amateurs and professionals each day and the glut of visual imagery is difficult to imagine.

Visual imagery triggers physical actions. Advertisers believe this and invest billions of dollars annually in media to shape consumer activity. In the same sense, suggestive and explicit images trigger many emotional, physical and spiritual responses. What we see prompts a response.

In his book *Popcultured* (InterVarsity Press, 2013, p. 20), Steve Turner cited filmmaker Paul Schrader's estimate that a thirty-year old person today in America has seen around 35,000 hours of audio-visual narrative. At the same age, the person's parents would have seen 20,000 hours; grandparents would have seen 10,000 hours, and great-grandparents 2,500 hours. "We are inundated by narrative," Schrader concluded. "We are swimming in storylines."

If the media was wholesome and even godly, we could make a better case for viewing it. Even then, however, at some point viewing media becomes a consummate time-waster chewing into the priorities and commitments needed for a successful life. Today's media is awash with sexually explicit and suggestive material.

What we see and what we hear affects us. If they didn't, the film and music industries would not spend so much money to reach us.

Satan was and still is subtle. He delights in deception and turning our own thoughts and reasoning against us. His queries prompted Eve to question God and His goodness. The Tempter's speech triggered something within Eve and led to actions that cost her Paradise. He does the same today.

There's an old saying that a picture is worth a thousand words. If that supposition is remotely correct, we are immersed with messages, ploys, gimmicks, innuendos, and lies. In its sheer volume, today's media—music, photos, video, social, games, and so forth—has overwhelmed this generation. This avalanche of sights and sounds has achieved what was what once thought impossible—the heightening and the dulling of senses at the same time.

It reminds me of the true story told by Wayne Cordeiro in *Jesus: Pure and Simple* (Bethany House, 2012, pp. 128-129). A certain African tribe learned how to catch ducks in a nearby river. Ordinarily, the ducks were too swift and distrustful to allow even the wiliest hunter to draw near them. Over time, the tribesmen tried one method after another to capture the ducks. Finally, they came across the use of pumpkins.

Pumpkins were placed in the river upstream and allowed to float down toward the flock of ducks. The cautious fowl at first were startled and flew away at the sight of the pumpkin. When the pumpkins passed, however, the fowl would return to their usual place in the river. Again, the pumpkins would be released up stream and again the ducks scattered. The pumpkins would be released again and again until the ducks no longer flew away but watched the pumpkins carefully as they floated by. Eventually, the ducks accepted the pumpkins as a normal part of life along the river and stopped noticing them at all.

When the hunters were confident that the ducks were no longer mindful of the pumpkins, they hollowed out the pumpkins, placed them over their heads and waded into the river. Floating in the midst of the accepting flock of ducks, the hunters pulled them under one at a time.

If we drop our defenses, we too are sitting ducks. The enemy placed a target on us a long time ago. He learned that the way to pull humanity down is through temptation. And the way to reach us is largely through sights and sounds. With these the enemy influences our behavior and dulls our consciences and sensitivity to the Spirit.

Temptation may be an old trick, but it has never been more formidable than in today's media-saturated culture.

Challenging the Status Quo

Amusement comes from two words meaning "without thought." Most people are thoughtless when it comes to responding to temptation. Without contemplation or examination, they simply go along with whatever the Tempter places before their eyes and ears.

It's the norm to go along without thinking; it's abnormal to stop and examine the situation first.

Jason's Story

He wasn't what you'd call "holier-than-thou," but he was known by his friends to be thoughtful and purposeful in his actions. The group had been together since elementary school and Jason's caution was well known. They teased him mercilessly as being timid and frightened. Regardless of what they wanted to do, he always had a question or a concern that they deemed to slow the group down from what it wanted to do.

While on a class trip in a nearby city, someone on a busy sidewalk handed a flyer to one of the group members advertising a movie being shown at little cost in a run-down part of town. It just so happened to be a movie a couple of them had been dying to see but the cost was prohibitive. The group was scheduled to be with their other classmates at an event during the same time, but since the attendees numbered into the hundreds those wanting to see the movie instead argued their absence would go unnoticed.

The majority of the group was leaning toward skipping the class event and going to the movie when Jason made an observation. "This sounds fishy to me." Immediately, the remainder of the group mocked Jason for his customary caution. But, for some reason, Jason fought back more than normal.

"Think about it, guys," Jason reasoned. "Why would they be showing this movie at such a reduced rate? And why would this movie be available in that part of town? At best, it's probably a knockoff of the original. At worst, there may be something else going on."

Not for the first time, the group stopped to argue with Jason. This time, however, Jason won the day. The group went to the class event and skipped the movie.

Days later, the discount movie ruse was revealed by the news media to be a setup. Unsuspecting moviegoers looking for a cheap movie showed up at the abandoned movie theater only to be beaten and robbed.

Sometimes, all it takes to challenge the Tempter is to stop and think about the matter a moment. Taking an opposite opinion among our peers may be a difficult thing to do, but quite often it is the action that silences the Tempter and avoids misfortune.

Do you remember King Jehoshaphat of Judah in Scripture? He was, by and large, considered a good king. He wasn't always wise in his associations and alliances, but his name is remembered well in the chronicles of the kings. On one occasion, Jehoshaphat enters into an alliance with Israel's King Ahab to defeat the enemy at Ramoth-Gilead (I Kings 22; II Chronicles 18). Jehoshaphat requests that Ahab first ask God if this battle was wise and in His plan. Ahab calls on his prophets—400 in all—and they prophesy that the Lord will deliver the enemy into his hand.

The prophets were unanimous in their bad advice. It just didn't feel right to Jehoshaphat, so he asked Ahab if there was not another prophet who could speak the Lord's mind and will. Ahab located his nemesis, the prophet Micaiah, who never told Ahab what he wanted to hear.

Micaiah is brought before the pair of kings. He indicated that a lying spirit had deceived the four hundred prophets. The battle was not going to go as they indicated. Ahab would perish. Micaiah's word proved true. Jehoshaphat would barely escape with his life and Ahab would be killed in battle.

It takes great courage to resist the temptation to go along with the crowd. Sometimes we will stand alone or nearly alone. We may be shunned and ridiculed. Yet, speaking truth to perceived power is what we do.

To do this requires flipping a mental and spiritual switch that says, "What God thinks matters more to me that all else around me," and acting accordingly. Jesus once prayed, "Not my will, but thine be done" (Luke 22:42). In that same sense we must accept the fact that our position may momentarily be that of the minority, but we play to an audience of One—One who sees all and rewards all.

Joseph is often called the "Jesus of the Old Testament." There are many similarities between Joseph and Jesus—both were favored, both experienced disowning and jealousy by their brethren, both of their lives were threatened by those near to them, and both ultimately arose from their trials to claim their rightful, divinely-ordained places.

Joseph has much to teach us about temptation—especially sexual temptation. The lady of the house where he worked, Potiphar's wife, set her eyes on Joseph. She determined to seduce him and pled with him to have sex with her. It was probably not uncommon in Egypt for this to happen. In fact, it may have been the accepted practice in the land. But Joseph did not answer to Egyptian culture. His culture was that of another land and place. He was in Egypt; but not of Egypt.

When Joseph refused Mrs. Potiphar's advance the final time, she concocted a story that he was the aggressor and that she was the victim. This willingness to defy the accepted norm purchased Joseph a long stay in prison. Joseph's biography is long in the Book of Genesis, but we never read that Joseph regretted his decision. In fact, his decision to stand against the temptation placed him eventually in a position where Pharaoh, ruler of Egypt, would call upon him.

Standing for truth may seem to bring defeat but it is only momentary. For anytime a person stands against the lies of the majority and speaks truth in love, a victory is coming in the future.

What prompted Joseph to stand? After all, the Ten Commandments had not yet been written—there was no seventh commandment prohibiting adultery. How did Joseph know what was right in the situation? And what gave him the power to withstand temptation and stand against the enemy's lies?

These questions are asked by a question posed by Joseph to Potiphar's wife, "How then can I do this great wickedness, and sin against God?" (Genesis 39:9). Joseph did not march to the music of the majority, but he followed the sound of a distant drummer. He listened to the still, small voice of God. His walk with God meant more to him than his approval by man.

The treatment Joseph received is instructive as well. He was lied about. He was mocked for his heritage and station in life, i.e., "this Hebrew servant" (Genesis 39:17). He was imprisoned and forgotten about by all but God.

Going against the grain of societal norms is not for the faint of heart. We have to make up our mind, "This is who I am and whose I am. I will withstand the enemy and I will stand for the Lord regardless of what it costs me."

The costs can be severe. For the three Hebrew children—Shadrach, Meshach, and Abednego—standing against the majority opinion led them to a fiery furnace. For Daniel's firmness to pray regardless of the king's decree, he was thrown in the lion's den. For Esther's fearless stand for her people, she risked her life entering the king's presence uninvited.

Being an anomaly requires courage. Each person who chooses to honor God with his or her lives will know when to face temptation or race from it.

Strategic Resistance

We know the enemy's devices. While temptations are many, the Tempter's approach is generally consistent:

- He first offers the bait. James said that each person is tempted "of his own lust" (James 1:14). In other words, the enemy knows our particular weaknesses and thereby knows how to fashion a unique situation that we find tempting.
- Next comes the internal appeal. Satan is not all-powerful, but he is very clever. If he offers the right bait, he knows there is a desire within us that will crave what he offers. Our thought-life is affected. We linger over it, trotting out endless scenarios and imaginations.
- The internal appeal leads to war within. The conscience and knowledge of the godly do war with the desires of the flesh. We may know it's wrong; we may even sense the pain it will cause. Yet, the flesh wars with the Spirit.
- Finally, we respond. Each temptation begins with bait and ends with a response. We resist or we yield; we win or we lose.

The temptations offered are many, but these generally fall in one of three categories: the lust of the flesh, the lust of the eye, or the pride of life (I John 2:16). Jesus faced each of these three temptations in His wilderness experience.

A few things are worthy to note about how our Lord faced temptation. The occasion is significant—Jesus was at His weakest after fasting for forty days without food. The Tempter came when Jesus was weakest physically. It's not unusual to find temptation to be the strongest when we are weakest. Many people confess that they fell to the Tempter when they were weary, depressed, hurt, disappointed, and discouraged. Yielding to temptations seem like a way of rewarding one's self when we feel mistreated or neglected.

Jesus faced a series of temptations. That seems important for us to understand. Just because you face one temptation does not mean you've faced them all. Temptations come regularly.

Finally, Jesus defeated these temptations with the Word of God. God's Word is powerful at all times, but when faced with a strong temptation His Word becomes all the more powerful. This suggests that temptation can find no room in our lives if we are filled with something more powerful.

Greg Smalley, marriage and family expert, was in a hardware store when understanding came to him about temptation. He had noticed weeds popping up in his yard and went to the store to get a bottle of weed killer. He doused the weeds and ended up killing healthy grass and the weeds came back. He tried again and achieved the same result. Finally, his wife told him to get some professional help before he killed the whole yard.

He found a lawn professional and asked him what to do about weeds. The man told Smalley that if you want a healthy yard, you don't go after the weeds. Your focus should be on the healthy grass. Once a lawn is healthy enough it will choke out the weeds. (Journal, "Rebuilding Marriage: Where Is the Hope?", 9/13).

It's that way with temptation. Developing healthy habits will do more to defeat temptation than to focus on the temptation itself.

Here's a list of things to try when the world offers us one assortment after another of temptations:

1. Know your weaknesses and when you are at your weakest (Proverbs 22:3).
2. Occupy your mind with God's thoughts and God's Word (Colossians 3:2).
3. Learn to pray powerfully and effectively (Hebrews 4:15-16).
4. Avoid places and people where you know you will be tempted (I Thessalonians 5:22).
5. Seek accountability partners (Ecclesiastes 4:9).

In the ancient Greek writings, strange creatures called sirens appeared to sailors. They inhabited coral-encrusted islands or rocky straits that were particularly hazardous to the ships. Sirens are usually depicted with the faces of women, the bodies of birds, and the voices of angels. Their songs were lovely, but ever so fatal.

Their melodious voices and near-angelic appearance caused the sailors to veer from the safe, deep-water channels and journey close to the dangerous islands. Just when it looked like their vessels would escape harm and be none the worse for the detour, the razor sharp shoals shredded the ships and the sailors' lives would be lost.

Similar voices are calling to us. The apostle Paul warned of "so many kinds of voices in the world" (I Corinthians 14:10). If we listen to these voices and respond, we too can make a shipwreck of our lives.

Two remedies for the sirens are found in classic literature. The first used restraints. Odysseus, the hero in Homer's *Odyssey*, had himself lashed to the mast in preparation for passing the island inhabited by sirens. The second is found in *The Argonauts,* when Orpheus picked up a harp and sang such a beautiful song that he drowned out the song of the sirens.

Restraints and refrains, although ancient remedies, seem to work well today.

To squelch the modern sirens, we need the songs of worship that come from setting our minds on heavenly things. We also need the restraints of taking into captivity every thought and putting to death earthly desires (Colossians 3:1-10). Together, these are effective means of protecting our purity in a decadent age.

Although the majority of people will give in to temptations, God seeks the anomaly—the Joseph who will not compromise his convictions. This is a commitment each of us must make: "I choose to see how close I can live to God rather than to the world."

Follow-Up Questions:

1. According to Genesis 3:6, with what sense did Satan tempt Eve?

_____

_____

_____

2. Since the Ten Commandments were not yet written, why did Joseph withstand the sexual advancement of Potiphar's wife?

_____

_____

_____

3. What are the four steps of the Tempter's approach?

_____

_____

_____

_____

4. What, according to I John 2:16, are the three categories of temptations?

_____

_____

_____

5. What are five things we can try to help us resists Satan's temptations?

_____

_____

_____

_____

_____

Journal Your Thoughts:

As you review this chapter, journal ways you have resisted temptations in the past and possible ways you can strengthen your resistance in the future.

_____

_____

_____

_____

_____

_____

_____

_____

_____

_____

_____

_____

_____

_____

_____

_____

_____

_____

_____

_____

_____

_____

_____

CHAPTER FOUR – DATING . . . GOD'S WAY

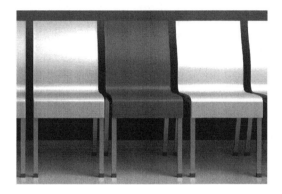

I want to tell you the world's shortest story.

A lamb walked into a lion's den.

Get the picture? That's really the only detail you need. You know what happens next, and you know the story doesn't end well. Sadly, it's a story told every day in our relationships. Where we go and who we're with will shape our world. We need to choose carefully. Our relationships are inseparable from our future. The people around us will either accelerate or incinerate God's plan for our life, which is why it's so important that we talk about dating.

A Dating Story

Listen to this story. A father sends his friend to another country in search of a bride for his forty-year-old son. There, the friend meets a young woman and asks her to marry the forty-year-old stranger. He essentially bribes her with a series of large gifts, and she agrees to the marriage proposal. She follows the man back home, where she is instantly married.

Sound bizarre? That's exactly what happened in the case of Isaac and Rebekah. Isaac's father, Abraham, sent his servant back to his hometown of Nahor. There, the servant prayed and God revealed Rebekah as Isaac's bride-to-be. He showered her with presents and then the proposal ensued. Rebekah's brother then posed the familiar question, "Wilt thou go with this man?" She consented and the journey to Canaan began.

Weddings like these have taken place for centuries. Families arranged their children's weddings, often while the children were still infants. A child could grow up knowing whom he would marry with no choice in the matter.

Times have changed, and we're all glad about it! During our mid-to-late teens, we usually begin dating, a process that will probably conclude with our selection of a mate and the beginning of a new family.

Dating is a bittersweet experience for most of us. Dating's downside is that it begins at the most awkward moment of our lives. This in-between stage is when we are neither a child nor an adult, but we undergo a crescendo of hormonal changes. Combine that factor with increased responsibility and career and college choices, and dating suddenly becomes one of life's most important events.

The interesting thing about dating is that it can make us extremely happy or it can leave us feeling utterly miserable. Dating done right can be a joyful learning experience. We can discover our own true selves, our tastes, our strengths, and our values. We can also discover the identity of our mate for life. Dating done wrong, however, can be deadly. It can leave us feeling confused, depressed, and defeated. That's why dating is a big deal.

There's a frightening tendency in modern dating relationships. Beginning as early as the mid-teen years, many of us begin to develop the tendency of fighting to save dating relationships as if we're trying to save a marriage that is falling apart. That's one of the reasons why single young adults in dating relationships are often some of the most stressed individuals you'll ever meet.

We all have those friends whose relationships are always full of drama and chaos. We watch the terrible cycle unfold. They find their "one true love" and are radiantly happy for a while. Then the fighting starts. Then they work it out. Then the fighting gets worse. They break up. Then they get back together, fight a little more, and finally end the relationship as mortal enemies.

Here's another one of those say-this-aloud moments.

I'm not going to marry everyone I date.

You won't. You can't. You're not supposed to because that's not how it works!

It may be hard to believe, but sometimes we're dating the wrong person. Sometimes God has someone better suited to us, someone who fits our life and our dreams better. But if we spend all our time fighting to love the wrong one, there's a great chance we'll miss the right one. Sometimes God's gift to our future is a door slammed in our face. His protection and direction often come disguised as pain. In an attempt to miss out on the pain of a relationship ending, many young adults tolerate relationships that aren't beneficial and aren't pleasing to God, and it's this desire to force a dating relationship to work that can derail the purpose of dating. When we have an improper view of the purpose of dating, we begin to tolerate things in a relationship that shouldn't be part of a healthy, godly relationship.

What we tolerate, we come to accept. What we accept, we learn to love. What we love, we will become. So we must be very, very careful what we tolerate.

If we tolerate sexual advances in dating, we'll grow to accept them. If we begin to accept them, we'll find ourselves wanting and needing them. And the cycle continues.

Dating has the potential to make us miserable, and if dating makes us miserable, we're doing it wrong. We can set ourselves free to love the right person instead of fighting to love the wrong one! We should not have to fight to make dating relationships last. If it doesn't work now, it certainly won't work later. If we have to force a relationship to work before we're married, we'll have to force it to work after we're married.

Godly dating serves many purposes. It teaches us how to be in relationships and how to mutually respect one another. It teaches us how to work out our disagreements. It teaches us what we're looking for (and often what we are not looking for) in a mate. Dating is much more than an innocuous pastime. It takes on supreme importance when we realize it leads to such a significant decision.

In dating, we should remember that our bodies are the temple of the Holy Ghost. We should submit our bodies to the Lord's control. During the dating years, we especially learn that self-control originates from a desire to please the holy, indwelling Spirit of Jesus Christ. If we approach dating and marriage with this attitude, we find it much easier to conquer temptations.

Three Types of Dates
Dates are usually of the following types: Casual, Curious, and Committed.

The Casual Date. This date can be with someone whom we've known for a long time or a short time. This type of date usually extends into early adulthood, has low emotional involvement, and almost always occurs in group settings with other people. The casual group date teaches us important things: rules of conversation, etiquette, and a better understanding of differing personalities.

The Curious Date. This date is with someone we want to get to know a little better. Generally, this "getting-to-know-you" type of date either escalates swiftly to a committed relationship date or digresses back to a casual group date. This type of dating can last for some time, especially if factors like distance, age differences, and more immediate goals exert influence. It's the kind of dating we think of when someone is spending time with another person without being in an exclusive relationship.

> *Chris and Carrie.* They met in the highly "unromantic" setting of elementary school. As classmates in third grade, they sat next to each other. At Valentine's Day, Chris presented Carrie

a valentine. Since that moment, each remained special to the other throughout the remainder of their childhood and adolescence. In separate colleges, each dated other people, but each knew that when the time was "right," something special would turn to something serious. On a summer's day, Carrie received the call she had expected for fifteen years. Chris had just earned a graduate degree and was "very interested" in seeing her. Within months, a third-grade valentine became a first-class wedding. Dates are like embers that can erupt into a forest fire at any moment!

The Committed Date. It goes by different names, but it generally involves an exclusive pairing-off between the dating couple. Trademarks of the committed relationship date are greater emotional involvement, time spent together, and the tendency for increased physical affection. The committed date is the logical progression of the dating process and is generally the precursor to engagement. For that reason, some people recommend that committed dating be practiced only by those people prepared for marriage. Say this aloud:

"Exclusive, steady dating can prevent us from getting the most from our young adult years."

Let that sink in.

> *Jeremy and Andrea.* Youth camp! Andrea loved youth camp. She lived for it each year. She had made friends with people across her state that she wrote or called on a regular basis. This summer, however, the thought of a looming youth camp didn't appeal to her. The reason was simple: Jeremy, her

steady boyfriend. There was no guy in particular that Andrea hoped to see at camp, yet there was this lingering feeling that she should be free to find out. Although she and Jeremy had an understanding that each could date others, any time it happened it was usually met with outbursts of rage and hurt. Andrea didn't feel like hearing, "How could you do this to me?" So, the weekend before camp, as much as she dreaded doing it, she told Jeremy that she didn't want to see him anymore. She was glad she did. The camp evangelist's son caught her eye and three years later they were husband and wife. Lengthy, exclusive dating can often blind a person to God's will.

Selecting a Date.

Worldly people select dates in a casual, indiscriminate way. Rolling the dice, some even respond to the tabloid, personal ads for companionship. In contrast, we should choose dates among believers in either our home church congregation or another congregation of like precious faith.

It is absolutely imperative that we date only those who share our faith and values. Some young adults argue that it is all right to have casual dates with those outside the church. They justify this by saying, "We're just friends," or "I'm trying to win them to the Lord." If we are sincere about pleasing God in all areas of our lives, then we will carefully screen all of our dates. Why? Because every date is a prospective mate.

We cannot predict with whom we will fall in love. Therefore, by controlling whom we date we limit those about whom we are eventually apt to care greatly.

There are two other considerations in selecting a date. First, our dates reveal our character. We might argue against the fairness of this assumption, but like it or not, we are known and judged by the company we keep. If we are serious about preserving our Christian testimony and influence, we will consider this before selecting a date. If we date someone who has been highly promiscuous, it speaks loudly about our own morality. Paul not only tells us to refrain from fornication (I Thessalonians 4:3), but he also commands us to refrain from even the appearance of evil (I Thessalonians 5:22).

The second consideration is that our dates influence our actions. Peer pressure affects us in our adolescent years more than at any other time. As much as we would like to think that we are the "captains of our fates, and the pilots of our destinies," others influence us.

At times, others influence us for good: "Iron sharpeneth iron; so a man sharpeneth the countenance of his friend" (Proverbs 27:17). Still, at other times, our peers influence us for bad: "Bad company corrupts good character" (I Corinthians 15:33, NIV). This is why God has always commanded His people to disassociate themselves from people who were displeasing to Him. We will be tomorrow what our friends are today.

Dating Different

What if you did dating differently? What if you broke the cultural mold of what society says dating should be and instead took the challenge of dating God's way?

Cancer tells the body it is present by seven danger signals. In the same sense, there are some danger signals that signify a destructive dating relationship.

Seven Danger Signals of an Improper Dating Relationship

1. When *spiritual things suffer,* like church attendance, prayer, and Bible reading
2. When we value our date's opinion more than the *opinions of our parents and pastor*
3. When our *personal standards* are laid aside while in the presence of our date
4. When we *cease wanting to be with others* and want to be exclusively with our date
5. When our *God-given goals and dreams* are put on hold for the sake of our date
6. When we habitually date *people much older* than ourselves
7. When we *attempt to justify* the lowering of sexual standards

Just as an artist must step back from the canvas to gain perspective, so we need to examine our dating relationships. If one or more of the above danger signals are present, we should seek godly counsel and seriously contemplate ending the relationship. Then, we should again secure life's greatest decision: putting God first in our lives.

Behavior on a Date

God wants us to be happy, but more than that, He wants us to be holy. There are few areas of life that provide as great an opportunity for holiness or the lack of holiness than in our relationships. We fulfill God's will when we live in a way that is pleasing to Him. Our bodies are the temple of God; and since dating involves our bodies, our conduct on a date is God's concern.

While fornication will bring temporary pleasure, it carries lifelong, even eternal, consequences. Since the threat of premarital sex is always present, we should place well-defined limits on physical affection. God commanded Israel to place battlements or parapets upon the rooftops to prevent anyone from plunging to their deaths or disfigurement (Deuteronomy 22:8). In a similar sense, we should put curbs on our dates. Here are a few to consider:

- Plan dates ahead. Any "un-planned" date generally follows the course of least resistance. Many bored teens have fallen victims to their poorly planned date. (See Proverbs 4:14-15.)
- Stick with the group. The next best thing to self-discipline is positive peer pressure. That's why we should date within the confines of a larger, godly group. (See Hebrews 10:25.)
- Stay in well-lit, public areas. While we may trust ourselves and our dates, the Book of Life teaches us to distrust both the flesh and the devil (Romans 13:14; Ephesians 4:27). Honorable activity in dating invites public disclosure. (See John 3:19.)
- Be accountable to parents. If our desire is to please God, then we should not resist parental authority. We should secure parental permission for our dates. We should also let them know where we are going, whom we will be with, and when we will be back.
- Set standards beforehand. Our parents and pastor can assist us in the formulation of limits to physical affection before we begin dating. Then, when tested on a date, we should seek to live up

to our personal code. A little planning in advance can prevent a disastrous fall in the future.

Retaining Vessels of Honor

Just as there were sacred vessels used in the Old Testament Tabernacle, so our bodies are set apart for God's use. Paul said that we should all know "how to possess" ourselves in a holy, honorable way. As with many other things, knowledge is power. The power to live above sin comes through knowing certain things. We can't be ignorant of three laws that threaten our decision to abstain from fornication: *the law of emotional progression, the law of diminishing returns, and the law of momentum.*

The *Law of Emotional Progression* teaches that physical acts trigger emotional responses and the more meaningful the physical act, the more intense the emotional response. Consider the following ladder of physical affection, starting with the bottom rung:

> Holding hands
> Light kissing (closed-mouthed kissing)
> Heavy kissing (open-mouthed kissing)
> Light petting (contact between neck and waist)
> Heavy petting (contact below the waist)
> Intercourse

In a dating relationship, we find greater emotional thrills elicited if we climb this ladder of physical affection. The emotional thrills encountered at one level tempt us to go farther.

Of course God's Word teaches us to abstain from lust, not only fornication, so before marriage we must stop at an early stage in this progression.

The *Law of Diminishing Returns* teaches us that the dating couple who advances to kissing isn't content to digress to the less intimate level of holding hands. When a couple reaches a specific level of affection, they may progress farther, but they will rarely, if ever, be content to go backwards. Also, it is common for a couple to move on to a higher level of affection since the former level no longer brings the desired excitement.

The *Law of Momentum.* Finally, the simple law of momentum says you can't stop something instantly. Since higher levels of physical affection bring greater emotional pleasure, and since we find decreasing pleasure at the same stages of physical affection, we steadily seek greater pleasure. The inexorable law of momentum says that things don't immediately stop once we decide to put on the brakes. In the interval when we realize we should stop and try to do so, some damaging distance can be covered.

Directing a Date

As with all laws, the law of emotional progression, the law of diminishing returns, and the law of momentum aren't changed, only respected. So we must use these laws to rightly guide our dating behavior.

Before Lot ended up in Sodom, the Bible says he looked in that direction (Genesis 13:10); then, he pitched his tent toward Sodom (Genesis 13:12). If Lot didn't want to go to Sodom, he shouldn't have gazed at it longingly or pointed his tent in that direction.

Gradually, but steadily, we move in the direction of our affections. Excessive display of affection, solitude, intoxicating substances, provocative clothing, and wrong dating partners all tend to point us towards premarital sex. Once we set our affections in this direction, the inexorable laws pull us towards a certain conclusion.

> I thought he was a nice boy! Cassia had never dated anyone quite like Derek. Five years older than she, he was so self-assured, yet so very personable. His dark hair, olive complexion, jutting jaw, and deep dimples made him look, if possible, like a rugged teddy bear. His nice manners and Cassia's insistence nudged her parents into permitting them to date. Their first few dates were innocent enough. Then, there came the cold night when he invited her up to his apartment for hot mug of cocoa. Cassia knew that no one else would be there and she would be violating one of her own dating policies: never be alone indoors with a guy. She thought that it wouldn't hurt to do it just once. Lulled by a cheery, roaring fire and her winsome, worldly-wise date, she succumbed to temptation. Shortly thereafter, Derek stopped seeing Cassia, leaving her with a load of guilt. The moral of the story: If you don't want to have premarital sex, don't start moving in that direction.

There are many specific ways to get a date pointed away from premarital sex. Below are ten ways that we can suitably direct a date.

Ten Ways to Direct a Date

1. Seek parental/pastoral approval on dates.

2. Avoid dating someone who is significantly older or who has a reputation for seeking premarital sex.

3. Pray before the date. Pray specifically that God gives you the strength to glorify Him in your body.

4. Make up your mind beforehand, "I will not have sex and will not intentionally do anything that will lead me to desire sex."

5. When you sense that your date desires to go too far, excuse yourself or change your environment.

6. Plan in advance what to do or say if things start going in the wrong direction.

7. Never go into homes without chaperones.

8. Avoid all intoxicating substances.

9. Communicate to parents in advance the time you will return and the place you will be.

10. Stay within a godly group.

Reasons Sex Is Worth the Wait

For Rebekah, the long journey to Canaan was worth the wait. At the end of the journey, her companion awaited her. In the same way, we maintain our sexual purity while waiting for Christ to bring the appropriate companion into our lives. That companion will be worth the wait.

Why should we wait until marriage for sexual intercourse? Here are a few reasons why sex belongs only in marriage:

- God blesses those who wait.
- Patience develops our walk with the Lord.
- Waiting enhances the probability of our marrying for the right reasons.
- Waiting until marriage for sex protects us from physical and emotional harm.
- Waiting preserves our Christian testimony.
- Waiting provides a good example to our future children.

Dating can be a great thing. It can be a valuable, important, and fun part of life if we date God's way. It enters our lives, however, at the inopportune moment when we are making choices on careers and colleges. Sometimes it's difficult to keep it all in proper perspective, but it's possible to keep dating on track. Dating can be an incredibly valuable experience provided we keep God at the center, keep our eye on the proper motives of dating, and commit to date the right way for the right reasons.

Always remember this:

When determining our beliefs about relationships and dating, remember that any decision that moves us further away from God is the wrong decision. The decision that moves us closer to Him is the right one. Always.

Follow-Up Questions:

1. True or False: I'm not going to marry everyone I date.

   _____

2. What are the three types of dates?

   _____

   _____

   _____

3. What are the seven danger signals of an improper dating relationship?

   _____

   _____

   _____

   _____

   _____

   _____

   _____

4. What are the six rungs on the ladder of physical affection, starting with the bottom rung?

   _____

   _____

   _____

   _____

   _____

   _____

5. List the ten ways we can suitably direct a date?

_____

_____

_____

_____

_____

_____

_____

_____

_____

_____

Journal Your Thoughts:

As you and your group read and study this chapter, journal how your concept of godly dating practices have been informed and strengthened.

_____

_____

_____

_____

_____

_____

_____

_____

_____

_____

_____

_____

_____

_____

_____

_____

_____

_____

_____

_____

_____

_____

CHAPTER FIVE –
EVERYONE'S CONNECTED

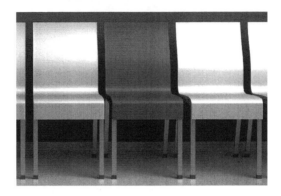

In 1929, Hungarian author Frigyes Karinthy proposed the idea that every person on the planet was no more than six relationships away from being connected to any other living person. Called "Six Degrees of Separation," the theory supposes that being "a friend of a friend" connects everyone on the planet within six steps. The concept has shown up in books, in movies, and even in a popular party game called "Six Degrees of Kevin Bacon." The game claims that all actors and actresses worldwide are within six connections of Hollywood actor Kevin Bacon.

A recent study by researchers at the University of Milan has determined that social media has reduced that number from six degrees of separation to four degrees of separation for roughly 93 percent of the world's population. Narrowing the parameters of the study to social media users within the same country reduces the number to an average of only three degrees of separation ("The Anatomy of Facebook," Lars Backstrom).

The point? Everyone is connected. If you don't believe it, just hang out in a crowd of people who follow you on social media. They don't even have to be close friends for you to get comments like this:

"Oh, weren't you just in Florida?"
"I love what you wore last Sunday!"
"I didn't know you had a dog!"
"Didn't you just get a new car?"
"I really like the color you painted your walls."
"Did you enjoy your vacation?"

Everyone is connected. Everyone knows everyone else. And like it or not, for better or worse, everyone knows what we're doing. We're all plugged in, and here's the thing:

We're powered by whatever we're plugged into.

If we're plugged into gossip, gossip will drive us. If we're plugged into immorality, we'll be immorality-driven. Our connections guide our tomorrow, and sadly, many of us, our peers, and our friends are making very dangerous connections.

The New Ugly

"14-Year-Old Girl Charged with Murder in Fatal Shooting of Chicago Teen"

The headline caught my attention, but the article broke my heart. It's the story of two girls arguing over a boy on Facebook. The social media feud escalated to a real-world confrontation on a sidewalk as they walked home from school. A fistfight broke out, a gun was pulled, shots were fired, and a fourteen-year-old girl lost her life because of a social media argument.

Another Internet search for crimes that had their root in social media turned up results that were staggering — dozens of murders, attempted murders, assaults, thefts, and kidnappings, each rooted in a social media interaction gone wrong.

If fashion has a new black, then connectivity has found its new ugly in electronic communication. Much of our electronic communication has become a vehicle that makes the delivery of meanness and hatred far too convenient. We say things online and in text messages that we would never say face to face. We do things in the electronic world that we would never do in the real one. It's not that social media and electronic communication has changed our hearts. It simply makes it easier for the truth about our hearts to shine through.

What's the truth about our hearts, you ask? The Gospel of Luke reminds us that our words overflow with the content of our hearts (Luke 6:45). Poisonous words reveal a poisonous heart. Loving words reveal a loving heart. Always.

The prophet Jeremiah talked about the nature of our hearts at length. "The heart is deceitful above all things, and desperately sick; who can understand it? I the Lord search the heart and test the mind, to give every man according to his ways, according to the fruit of his deeds" (Jeremiah 17:9-10 ESV).

In life as in nature, diseased fruit sometimes points to a diseased root, and by the time bitterness blossoms, the tree is often corrupted beyond salvage. On the other hand, by the time a tree bears healthy fruit, it has seen enough growth and faithful nourishment to support its fruitfulness. The fruit we bear is an inevitable result of the health or infirmity of our private world. Fruit never lies. Never. Never.

Before you go any further, take a minute and take a heart inventory. What's inside your heart? What comes out in your thoughts, words, and actions? What grows in the fertile soil of your heart?

I'm Right, You're Right, We're All Right, Alright?

In 2011, Marist College in Poughkeepsie, New York, took a poll of the most annoying words to hear used in daily communication. Near the top was the constant interjection of the word "like." That's, like, so totally obvious. Another popular entry was the equally meaningless concluding phrase, "you know what I mean." Which one took the prize as the worst word? Almost 40 percent of the more than 1,000 respondents agreed the most grating, obnoxious thing you can hear in a conversation is the word, "whatever."

Whatever. Only three syllables, but they say so much. "I don't care. I don't believe you. This doesn't matter to me. Your priorities aren't mine."

Mom: If you do that, you're going to get in trouble!
Son: Whatever.
Mom: You know I love you.
Son: Whatever.
Mom: You'll thank me later!
Son: Whatever.

Few other single words can communicate such hostility in three syllables.

The modern distrust of absolute truth has developed into a social "whatever" attitude. In this environment, anything goes and modern culture encourages the adoption of a live-and-let-live attitude toward other people. What is true for one, they reason, might not be true for another. Whatever you want to do is alright for you, even if it's not right for me. You want to wear a unicorn costume every day? Whatever. You want to marry a mailbox? Whatever.

The rules are being rewritten every day, and they are governed by a "whatever." George Barna, the noted Christian analyst and statistician, describes the rules of this generation.

1. Personal relationships count. Institutions don't.
2. The process is more important than the product. How you get there is more important than where you go.
3. Aggressively pursue diversity among people.
4. Enjoying people and opportunities is more important than achievement.
5. Change is good.
6. The development of character is more crucial than achievement.
7. You can't always count on your family to be there for you.
8. Each individual must assume responsibility for his or her own world.
9. Whenever necessary, gain control.
10. Don't waste time searching for absolutes. There are none.
11. One person can make a difference in the world—but not much.
12. Life is hard and then we die. Enjoy it.
13. Spiritual truth may take many forms.

14. Express your rage.
15. Technology is our natural ally.

(George Barna, *Generation Next*)

The tenth and thirteenth rules on the list just about say it all, don't they?

Don't waste time searching for absolutes. There are none. And spiritual truth may take many forms. They're scary ideas, but we see them lived out around us daily.

It's this type of culturally-bred distrust that leads to moral and spiritual chaos. If I decide absolute truth is a myth, then my concept of right and wrong gets its definition from flesh and I can convince myself that what feels right to me must be right. It's a dangerous, "whatever" way to live.

Feeling-driven morality always ends in immorality. Flesh doesn't like rules, and when flesh begins to make our decisions, we always move toward the boundaries of right and wrong.

It's far easier to love God's principles in theory than to live out God's practices in reality. It's possible to attend church, be involved, sing in the choir, teach Sunday school, say I'm a Christian, and then embrace evil communication as soon as we walk out the doors.

Connection 2.0

Evil communications corrupt good manners (I Corinthians 15:33). Let's look at some trends in damaging, high-interaction, low-commitment connections. Their momentary nature is their defining characteristic, and they tend to result in the corruption of kindness and goodness.

Texting/Sexting

An average of six billion text messages are sent each day around the world, which equals about two trillion messages per year. According to Pew Research Center, 97 percent of people under age forty-four use cell phones daily to talk or text. Of those six billion texts, an increasing number of them are sexually explicit. Sexting, the sending of explicit messages, photos, or videos via text message is increasing yearly. Closer to home, in a recent study of Apostolic young adults, 34 percent of respondents admitted to sending provocative or nude photos via text message.

Perhaps it's the seeming safety of distance, or the low-commitment nature of the communication, but sexting is a constant reminder of what the American Psychological Association calls the "sexualization of America." It's a brand new battle that wasn't fought as recently as a few years ago. Most frighteningly of all, it is increasing in popularity among early adolescents (Tami Verhelst, National Institute for Trauma and Addiction Professionals).

Social Media

Similarly, the one-way communication of social media has changed the way the world shares information. Conversation is no longer necessary for communication. I can tell you about my day, what I had for lunch, and what I'm doing tonight without any feedback from you. It's a great way for me to inform you of my activities, but it's a terrible basis for relationship.

Social media tends to be a lot of talking and very little listening. James 1:19 tells us we should be quick to hear and slow to speak, while social media tells us exactly the opposite. The problem that creates is that so much of the Christian lifestyle revolves around us hearing the voice of God clearly, and it appears social media is teaching many of us to talk more than we listen. Couple that with the frequently negative viewpoints shared, the opportunity for communication without accountability, and the tendency to behave electronically in ways we would never behave in reality, and it's a deadly communication combination.

The best example of the power of the virtual world is in the simple fact that over a billion dollars is spent each year buying artificial things in artificial online social media games—virtual shovels for virtual farms, or virtual pets to populate your virtual house. There's nothing wrong with playing a game. But there's something very wrong when the virtual world begins to get more attention than the real one.

Social media is not inherently bad, but flesh is. The Bible says that flesh lusteth to envy. Our humanity is drawn to the bad, the scandalous, and the negative. Like a drug, evil communication can be the soul's morphine, and social media can be the needle in the vein.

Friends with Benefits
It's not new to the twenty-first century, but it does create some twenty-first century problems. Call it friends with benefits, or sexual partners without relationship, but it's a symptom of the same one-way communication sickness. "Friends with benefits" is another way of saying, "it's about me getting what I want."

The "friends with benefits" concept doesn't stop at heterosexual relationships. Perhaps it's due to the increased visibility of homosexual behavior in media, but there is simultaneous increase in homosexual experimentation among friends. In a survey of Apostolic young adults, over 10 percent admitted to at least one sexual encounter with a member of the same sex. In online discussion regarding same sex experimentation, there's a recurring theme of "I'm not gay; I'm just curious."

The broader theme of low-commitment sexual partners, both heterosexual and homosexual, is that sex is simply a game. The problem with sex outside marriage is that it's the only game where everyone loses.

What's the common thread between sexting, social media, and friends with benefits? They're all momentary connections that have woven their way into the fabric of our society, and our relationship with them is a sign of the decay of our personal boundaries.

Life Lessons from a Lawnmower

In late childhood, it's not uncommon to begin helping with yard work. I can still remember some of the first times I was allowed to climb on the riding lawnmower and take a ride around the back yard to cut the grass. In adulthood, it's just work, but in childhood it seemed like so much fun.

Our property line was next to a vacant lot that was overgrown with brush and undergrowth. Pine trees constantly dropped their needles and pinecones down on the tall grass below. Ugly weeds filled the lot from front to back and side to side, and it was my job to make sure the distinction between our lot and that lot was clear.

When it was my turn to drive the lawnmower, I always loved riding down that property line and cutting back the tall weeds that grew across it. I loved the smell of the cut grass, the sound that the lawnmower made as I rumbled down that boundary at a blazing five miles per hour. It wasn't really that big of a task, but it felt important to me.

As I've gotten older, I've realized it was very important indeed. Though I didn't realize it at the time, I was learning a valuable bit of truth about life. I knew where the line was, but the weeds didn't care. And it didn't matter how many times I cut them back, within a couple weeks, they were growing taller and creeping back across my line. The lines and boundaries of a life lived for Jesus Christ are no different. I learned a really important lesson that has remained in my mind for most of my life. If you want a line to stay clear, you have to keep cutting down the weeds.

Matthew 13 tells the story of a man and his wheat field. Under the cover of darkness, an enemy sneaks in and plants weeds in the middle of the wheat. If I could only pick one parable from the Bible to illustrate the relationship between the Christian lifestyle and the carnal one, this would be it. Life constantly plants weeds along your boundary lines. Tares grow in the middle of what should be a healthy harvest. And if you want to maintain the health of your field, you have to deal with the tares.

As an eleven year old, when I saw the weeds growing high, it meant it was time to go fire up the lawnmower and redraw some boundaries. Now that I'm older, it's not about the lawnmower anymore, but it remains wholly about the boundaries.

Rebuild the Wall

Time and proximity often blind us to the slow decay of personal boundaries. Tend and mend your fences. Any wall worth having is worth repairing.

The first six chapters of the Book of Nehemiah record the prophet Nehemiah's quest to rebuild the walls of Jerusalem. The City of God sat in ruins. Its walls were pulled down and its gates destroyed, and one man decided he was going to do what God called Him to do and secure the city once again from its enemies.

He faced obstacles both inside and outside the city. The construction took time, persistence, and dedication. But the City of God was ruined without some walls to keep it safe.

If a rebuilt wall can secure the future of a city, a rebuilt wall can secure the future of a life. It may be a difficult process. Anytime you try to do the right thing, chances are an enemy will come knocking on your door. In Nehemiah's story, it was Sanballat and Tobiah who were determined to see him fail.

Here's a news flash for you. Everybody who knows your name is not your friend. Everybody who sends you a friend request doesn't have your best interests at heart. There may be a Sanballat and Tobiah waiting right now to see you fall. In order for you to make the right connection with your purpose, there may be some wrong connections you need to break.

You need to write down the next few sentences on a sticky note and put it somewhere you can see it every day:

Every relationship is not a healthy one, and life is not a contest to see who can collect the most followers. If you have friends who gossip about others with you, rest assured they gossip about you when you're not with them. Repeat after me: Unfollow, unfriend, delete. To get where you need to go, you may need to lose a few phone numbers, friends, followers, and followees. Nothing is more damaging to spiritual health than the constant influence of carnal, cynical "friends." Your relationships shape your future. So make sure there aren't "wall breakers" with access to your life. You need to surround yourself with people who can encourage you to keep doing what God said do, to keep building, to keep cutting down the weeds, to keep drawing the boundary, and to keep living the life for which you were created.

God calls us to go deeper, higher, and further. If we are drifting shallower, lower, and backward, it's time to question whose voice we're following. We must guard our heart; guard our ears, guard our thoughts, and guard our actions.

In the crowded, crazy roar of life, there are a thousand voices speaking at any given moment. We need to make sure our ears are tuned to hear His still, small voice through it all. We need to tune out the noise. His is the voice that matters. That's the voice whose call can change everything.

Follow-Up Questions:

1. According to Luke 6:45, from what do our words overflow?

_____

_____

_____

2. According to Jeremiah 17:9-10, what is deceitful above all things?

_____

_____

_____

3. What is meant by this statement: "It's far easier to love God's principles in theory than to live out God's practices in reality"?

_____

_____

_____

4. How does the story of Sanballat and Tobiah tell us that everybody who knows our name is not our friend?

_____

_____

_____

5. Are there any friends you need to unfollow, unfriend, and delete?

_____

_____

_____

Journal Your Thoughts:

After reading this chapter and realizing how interconnected you are with the rest of the people of the world, journal how you can develop friendships and relationships with other people that will enhance your relationship with God.

_____

_____

_____

_____

_____

_____

_____

_____

_____

_____

_____

_____

_____

_____

_____

_____

_____

_____

_____

_____

CHAPTER SIX – THE COMMITMENT TO BE DIFFERENT

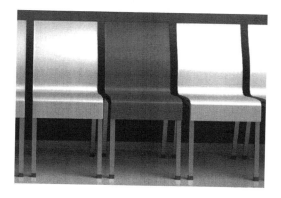

Indifferent

Americans love labels. We label anything and everything. One of our favorite things to label is generations. Those who lived and fought in the Second World War are called "The Greatest Generation." The ones who followed this war were called "Baby Boomers." Then came "Generation X," "Generation Y," "Millennials," and so forth.

If there was a single word that describes our generation — not just of teens and young adults, but also increasingly of all ages — it is "indifferent." Deluged by media, confronted with huge moral shifts, undermined by economic woes, and overwhelmed by global tragedies, many just seem to be growing increasingly apathetic. The prevailing attitude is one of malaise where people are asking, "Does it really matter anymore?"

Historically, indifference is one step from destruction.

In *The Town beyond the Wall*, Elie Wiesel tells the story of Michael, a young Jewish man in his thirties who survived the holocaust and purposes to journey behind the Iron Curtain to where he was raised. Michael remembered how he and his loved ones were brutalized, but his trip is not to extend forgiveness or to extract revenge. He went to satisfy a simple curiosity: "How a human being can remain indifferent."

Michael didn't have trouble grasping the hatred of his prison guards and the executioners. He had no trouble understanding hatred, ugly and ill-conceived as it was. He didn't understand, however, the one he called the "spectator," the person who watched through a window day after day as thousands of Jews were loaded into a death train. That face perplexed him. It contained no pity, no shock, no anger, and no interest. It was merely indifferent.

Wiesel concludes his story of Michael by asserting that "Evil is human, weakness is human; indifference is not."

As with the person suffering from frostbite in the Arctic, in danger of loss of limb and life, indifference indicates the end is near.

Indifference is the *zeitgeist*, the spirit of the age.

- Children are regularly exposed to pornographic images through the Internet. Yet, where is the outcry?
- Human trafficking is a huge multibillion-dollar criminal industry. Globally, the average cost of a slave is $90. Eighty percent of trafficking

involves sexual exploitation. The average age a teen enters the sex trade in the United States is from twelve to fourteen years of age. There are thousands of people trafficked into the United States each year (*www.dosomething.org*, "11 Facts about Human Trafficking"). When William Wilberforce fought slavery in the British Empire centuries ago, he said, "You may choose to look the other way but you can never say again that you did not know." Are we so indifferent?

- Sexually transmitted diseases run rampant in America, with young women being the most vulnerable. The Centers for Disease Control state that young people aged fifteen to twenty-four will acquire nearly half of all new STDs ("STDS in Adolescents and Young Adults", *www.cdc.gov*).
- Because of the digital revolution, an epidemic of pornography has swept the United States. It's estimated that 68 percent of young men and 18 percent of young women use porn at least once a week (Pornography Statistics, *www.covenanteyes.com*).
- Traditional marriage has fallen by the wayside through adultery, divorce, and the proliferation of same sex unions and marriages. To speak out against any of these is to be politically incorrect, so people remain silent. Is our silence nothing but indifference in disguise?
- The birth rate of single women continues to increase amongst all demographics (Census Bureau's American Community Survey).

- Almost half of first babies in United States are born to unwed mothers ("Knot Yet: The Benefits and Costs of Delayed Marriage in America").
- Unwanted pregnancies and abortions proliferate. Half of pregnancies among American women are unintended and about four in ten of these are terminated by abortion. About one in five abortions in America are from girls in their teens and about one in three abortions are from women ages twenty to twenty-four. ("Induced Abortions," *www.guttmacher.org*).

Tolerance is the supposed liberating message of the hour. We are told to, "Mind our own business." "Don't get involved." "Live and let live." "To each their own." And we are asked, "What does it matter to you?"

The coarsening of our culture should require a response on the part of the righteous. When the night grows darker, the light should burn brighter.

Yet, the broad path that leads to destruction allows no dissent. It insists upon conformity. There is no bucking the trend, no fighting the tide, no swimming against the current permitted. To get along, you must go along.

In Ephesians 2:1-9, the apostle Paul describes what it is like to follow the majority opinion. We were once dead due to our disobedience (v. 1). We followed the "course of the world" and obeyed the devil—the commander of the dark world (v. 2). We followed the passionate desires of our sinful nature and were subject to God's anger because of it (v. 3).

In other words, the indifference came from deadness. Perhaps this is why the risen Lord in the Book of Revelation desired that the church of Laodicea were hot or cold. Hot on fire for God is good. Cold in the Lord is not good, but workable. What God hates is the awful in-between state of being neither cold nor hot.

Indifference is a synonym to lukewarmness.

Someone has to care. Someone has to take a stand.
Martin Luther stood and changed the course of religion in Europe and the world.
Rosa Parks stood and changed her world.
Martin Luther King Jr. stood and changed his world.
Someone has to care. Someone has to take a stand.
Esther took a stand to protect her people.
Simon Peter stood on the Day of Pentecost to proclaim salvation.
Shammah stood in a patch of lentils and stayed until victory came.
Someone has to care. Someone has to take a stand.

Indifference will not be defeated until someone purposes to be the difference. That commitment is necessary to withstand in this indifferent age.

Dare to Be Different
How different should we be? The answer is, "Very different."

Let's cover a few passages of Scripture to show you how different God expects us to be.

God's Word describes us as His "peculiar people" (I Peter 2:9). In today's language, peculiar means someone who is strange, odd, or uncommon. Yet, it can also mean belonging exclusively to someone or something. Another way to say this is that God calls us to be His own "special people" or His "unique possession."

Each of us belongs to someone or something. Paul said that we are called to belong to the Lord Jesus Christ (Romans 1:6). We were once slaves to this world, but now we are love slaves—servants of choice—to our Lord (Romans 6:20-22).

At Calvary, Jesus Christ purchased us with His own blood (Acts 20:28). We no longer belong to ourselves. We gave up our rights. We were bought with a price (I Corinthians 6:19-20).

Let's back up a verse now and hear what Paul has to tell us.

> *Flee sexual immorality. Every sin that a man does is outside the body, but he who commits sexual immorality sins against his own body"* (I Corinthians 6:18, NKJV).

Paul's audience was in general to "all who in every place call on the name of Jesus Christ our Lord," but in particular he wrote to the "church of God which is at Corinth, to those that are sanctified in Christ Jesus, called to be saints" (I Corinthians 1:2).

Corinth, located in a strategic crossroads of Greece, was no picnic. Gordon Fee described Corinth as the "New York, Los Angeles and Las Vegas of the ancient world." Fee didn't mean this in terms of architecture or economics, but in terms of sinfulness. Corinth was quite simply the "Sin City" of its day.

To make it worse, the overt sexuality of the city was entwined with its religious diversity. At least twenty-six temples were considered sacred in Corinth and many involved ritualized prostitution.

So, when Paul wrote to his audience in Corinth he was addressing new converts trying to live differently than the culture in which they found themselves. Paul addressed numerous areas, but none so relevant as understanding that they were to be saints—separated from this world to God. This devotion, this voluntary act of worship, included dedicating their bodies to the Lord as His rightful possession. Paul said to them as he says to us, "Your body is the temple of the Holy Spirit. . . . Therefore glorify God in your body, and in your spirit" (I Corinthians 6:19-20).

Glorifying God in Body and Spirit

It's interesting to notice that Paul placed body before spirit, the outward man before the inward man. This is the same order also found in II Corinthians when Paul told the church to come out from the world and to cleanse themselves from "all filthiness of the flesh and spirit, perfecting holiness in the fear of God" (II Corinthians 7:1).

We live in a religious world where people say, "It's only what's on the inside that matters." Yet, in speaking to a promiscuous culture, Paul urged believers to focus not only on the inside, but to focus first on the outside. The apostle knew what we know today—unless there's a change in our daily lifestyle, there will be no lasting change within. Unless we're willing to immediately address the shortfalls of our outward man, there is simply little willingness to address the inward man.

When Jesus calmed the raging seas, He rebuked the wind first and then the waves. He addressed the cause and then the effect. Paul seems to suggest to the Corinthians that in a highly toxic culture and especially among new converts, spiritual slippage is noticed first in fleshly habits and practices.

We shouldn't overemphasize the exterior, but neither should we disregard what Paul teaches here. The words "modest" and "good behavior" used by Paul in his first letter to Timothy (2:9; 3:2) originate from the same Greek word, *kosmios*, meaning "well-ordered in his earthly citizenship." Our inward and outward man should be consistent. We should be a hearer and a doer.

To be different, both the outside and the inside need to change.

So, what needs to change on the outside?

- Our appearance needs to be modest, godly, and gender distinctive.
- Our amusements should be measured and wholesome.
- The places we go and do not go should bring glory to God.
- The company we keep should be wholesome.
- The music we hear, the media we watch, and the time we spend doing it should be radically different from this world.
- Habits such as prayer, reading the Bible, church attendance and involvement in ministry should displace habits that do not bring glory to God.

- We should cease to live for ourselves and be consumed with living for God and others.
- Our conversation and behavior should change.
- We should not be caught up in the pursuit of prestige, popularity, and prosperity. Rather, we should be caught up in doing the will of God.

What needs to change on the inside?

- Reorder our loves: God first, others second, and ourselves last.
- Love God fervently.
- Our thought life needs an overhaul—a renewing of our mind.
- Imagination—the most powerful and yet potentially destructive movie theater in the world—needs to be brought into line with God's Word.
- The fires of rebellion must be extinguished.
- Our will needs to be lost in God's will.
- We need to be filled continuously with the Holy Spirit.
- The fruit of the Spirit needs to grow unhindered in our life.
- Our dreams need to be channeled in God's direction.
- We need to relinquish our rights and give our heart, soul, and mind completely to the Lord.
- We need to make up our mind that we are different and will be the difference in the lives of others.

Today, we will be called to make that choice. Today, we will decide.

The root of the word "decide" is –*cide*, meaning to kill. It's the same root word of pesticide and genocide. When we decide, it means we've examined all of our options and chosen the one that will live and all others will be buried. If all the options but one have not been extinguished, then we cannot truly say, "I have decided."

We can choose to live in the many ways pleasing to the world or we can decide to follow God's way. It's an exclusive choice. It's a decision.

The Story of Francis of Assisi

Perhaps, you've heard the story told of a young man named Francis. Like Jacob of old, he wrestled with God and with himself.

On the winter's eve of taking his vows into a religious order, Francis made his way out into a snowy field. He loved a gracious and noble woman, but on the morrow, he would forever have to give her up. Tonight, something had to be done.

He fashioned from snow seven images—those representing his wife, children and servants. He arranged them in a circle and sat with them pretending for that moonlit evening the life he could have outside his calling. For the moment, he lost himself in a life that would never be his—one of ease and joy.

Someone overheard Francis talking to his make-believe wife and family. What he spoke may always be a mystery, but it's easy enough to figure that he was explaining his decision—telling the woman of his dreams of his great love for God and how he must serve the Lord alone.

Then, as the sun rose on his new life, he kissed each of the snow figures and bid them adieu. Turning his back on his own will, Francis followed after God's will.

That night, Francis conducted his own funeral. He died to all else but the will of God.

(Sources: F. W. Boreham, *Luggage of Life* and John Herkless, *Francis and Dominic and the Mendicant Orders*).

The commitment to be different is like conducting one's own funeral.

Are you ready to do the same?

The Commitment

"Set your affections on things above," Paul said, "and not on things on the earth" (Colossians 3:2).

Our hope comes from Heaven. Our help comes from the heights. Today, we lift our eyes up beyond the skies of blue into the realm where God reigns supreme. And we ask God to send a radiant shaft of light into our hearts and minds. Only in His presence does lasting change come.

We follow the same well-worn path that the risen Lord gave to the church at Ephesus who had left her first love. Jesus told them to "remember . . . repent . . . and repeat the first works" (Revelation 2:5).

First, we remember. Everything we've talked about to this point has been designed to stir up your memories. You should remember the character of God. You should remember how good and gracious He is.

He does not ask you to do anything He has not already done Himself. He lived a pure, spotless, sacrificial life and gave it at Calvary. He is the One who willingly laid His life down for you and me. He is the One who loves all those who have failed. His mercy endures forever.

Can you remember the first time you felt His presence? Do you remember when you knew regardless of whom else did or did not love you that God loved you? God cared for you then and He still does today.

If you have left your Heavenly Father, He still awaits your return, the return of the prodigal. The lights are burning. Your "Welcome Home" party is being prepared. He's looking down the road you left by, believing that you will come back.

There's a student ministry group longing to welcome you home. There are some friends you walked away from that long to wrap their arms around you. There's a sword and a shield waiting for you to lift them again. There's a breastplate of righteousness that God wants to restore.

"Remember from where thou art fallen. . . ."

Second, we repent. Sin is missing the mark. Repentance is admitting we missed the mark and doing a one-eighty.

When it comes to living a changed life, all of us must admit that we've not measured up. When it comes to sexual sins, many of us cannot say that we've been perfect. What should we do?

Listen to the psalmist: "Blessed be the name of the LORD from this time forth and forevermore" (Psalm 113:2). You can't do anything about yesterday except repent—nail it to Calvary's cross. But, from this moment forward you can live differently. You can hear God's voice saying, "Go and sin no more."

There are other voices speaking today. They say what they've always said:

- "You can't do this. You're a failure."
- "God doesn't love you."
- "You're a hypocrite."
- "If you do this, you will look foolish."
- "Why try? You're just going to fall again."

Yet, all of Heaven waits to rejoice over one person who repents. All of Heaven stands at attention at this moment waiting for you to say, "God, I need to start over."

Regret is good; repentance is better. For when you repent, you're getting pointed in the right direction. More important than your location is the direction in which you're pointed.

Third, we repeat the first works. What does that mean? It means we go back to what we did when we first loved the Lord.

We didn't care what others thought about us. We were lost in the newness of it all. Old things had passed away and we faced a brand-new world with limitless possibilities. We tuned out the chatter of those who were mindlessly following the world; we tuned into the Heaven and waited to hear from Him.

Back then, we longed to be in His presence. We longed to read His Word. We longed to be around God's people and to be all God would have us to be.

We made sure that God came first. That was our first love.

Today, we can get it all back. God is restored to His rightful place and we are restored to the heavenly places. If you've messed up, this is your day to start fresh.

The Reminder in Blue. God told the children of Israel to sew a blue ribbon or cord around the fringes of their garments. That ribbon was there for them to look at or to "catch their eye." A glimpse of blue ribbon while looking down was supposed to remind them to resist following after their own lusts, and to remember Heaven's wishes for their lives (Numbers 15:37-41).

The color blue was not unusual to the Israelites. The house of God was draped in blue; its furnishings were covered with blue material while in transit (Exodus 36:11; Numbers 4). When God's people placed a blue ribbon at the hems of their garments, they were reminded that they were Heaven's temple on earth. When they glanced down, the blue ribbon seemed to speak to them saying, "You aren't living for this world; you're living for a world to come."

There's an old saying for the proper attire of a bride on her wedding day:

> *Something old, something new,*
> *somthing borrowed, somthing blue.*

Blue is a symbol of the heavens. It symbolizes true and lasting love.

Perhaps you found a blue ribbon in this book or were given one by your pastor, teacher, or student ministry pastor.

A similar blue ribbon has been used by tens of thousands of teens and young adults who made a commitment to be different—to cling to moral purity while others trample it beneath their feet. While holding the blue ribbon, these have confessed that they are ambassadors on loan to this world. They are citizens of another world living momentarily in this world. They are change agents that should transform their world, not conform. They don't live for themselves; they live to please God.

This ribbon should remind you that God wants you to live pure in a toxic world. Heaven will bless those who patiently wait for Him and seek His face. To those who keep themselves sexually pure until their wedding days, God gives great grace and strength. To those who have made mistakes but desire to start over, there's new hope and new life for you.

With this blue ribbon in hand, make this pledge:

My pledge to God: From this day forward, I pledge to submit myself to Your will and to Your Word. I pledge to glorify you in my dating relationships. I will be careful whom I date and what

I permit on that date. I commit myself to inward purity in the privacy of my own mind and time. I commit myself to sexual purity, refraining from sex until I marry my God-given, lifelong companion.

My pledge to my future mate: I pledge to abstain from sex from this day until we marry. I will pray daily that God brings you—the person of His choice—into my life in His own time and way. This blue ribbon signifies my devotion to purity and to you. I will keep this blue ribbon with me or near me until our marriage. It will be that "something blue" that I bring to our wedding day.

My pledge to the world: I pledge to the world that I will be a light in your darkness. I will not listen to your lies but will hold on to Truth. I will be prayed-up and filled-up with the Spirit. I will always be ready to give reason for why I live as I do. I will be different so you too can be different. I will hold on to Heaven and help you escape Hell.

The Difference

You're different. You have to get comfortable with the fact that you've made a big commitment—the kind of commitment that is only possible if God is in it. But with Him, all things are possible and through Him, you can do all things.

The commitment to be different will be tested day-in and day-out. You must preserve the difference through prayer, God's Word, and through living and walking in the Spirit.

Culture says otherwise. Culture says it's impossible. Culture says this commitment is just a phase you're going through.

But when did culture gain the right to define the children of God?

You're different. You're a citizen of a different kingdom. You play by different rules. You're the child of another world, and as such, you're living to please God. By the standards of this world, that's odd. But by the standards of Heaven, odd is good.

You are different.
You are Apostolic.
You are an anomaly.
And there's absolutely nothing wrong with that.

Follow-Up Questions:

1. According to the authors, what single word describes our generation?

_____

2. Where did the indifference of Ephesians 2:1-9 originate?

_____

_____

_____

3. Identify five people listed in the lesson who cared enough to stand for right.

_____

_____

_____

_____

_____

4. In II Peter 2:9, what is meant by the words "peculiar people"?

_____

_____

_____

5. Consider the two lists toward the end of the chapter: "What needs to be changed on the outside?" and "What needs to be changed on the inside?" Are there areas that draw your interest as needing attention as you commit yourself to God in a greater manner?

_____

_____

_____

Journal Your Thoughts:

As you come to the end of this study, journal the development of your desire to submit to God and sexual purity, refraining from sex until you marry your God' given, lifelong companion.

_____

_____

_____

_____

_____

_____

_____

_____

_____

_____

_____

_____

_____

_____

_____

_____

_____

_____

_____

_____

_____

_____

_____

_____

_____